KNOPF
75
YEARS·OF·PUBLISHING

THE
NEW YORKER
BOOK OF CAT CARTOONS

THE
NEW YORKER
BOOK OF CAT CARTOONS

ALFRED A. KNOPF  NEW YORK 1994

THIS IS A BORZOI BOOK
PUBLISHED BY ALFRED A. KNOPF, INC.

Library of Congress Cataloging in Publication Data

The New Yorker book of cat cartoons.
p.   cm.
ISBN 0-394-58795-2
1. Cats—Caricatures and cartoons.   2. American wit and humor,
Pictorial.   3. New Yorker (New York, N.Y.)   I. New Yorker (New York, N.Y.)
NC1428.N47   1990
741.5'973—dc20   90-53070
CIP

Manufactured in the United States of America

Published October 25, 1990
Reprinted Nine Times
Eleventh Printing, November 1994

THE
NEW YORKER
BOOK OF CAT CARTOONS

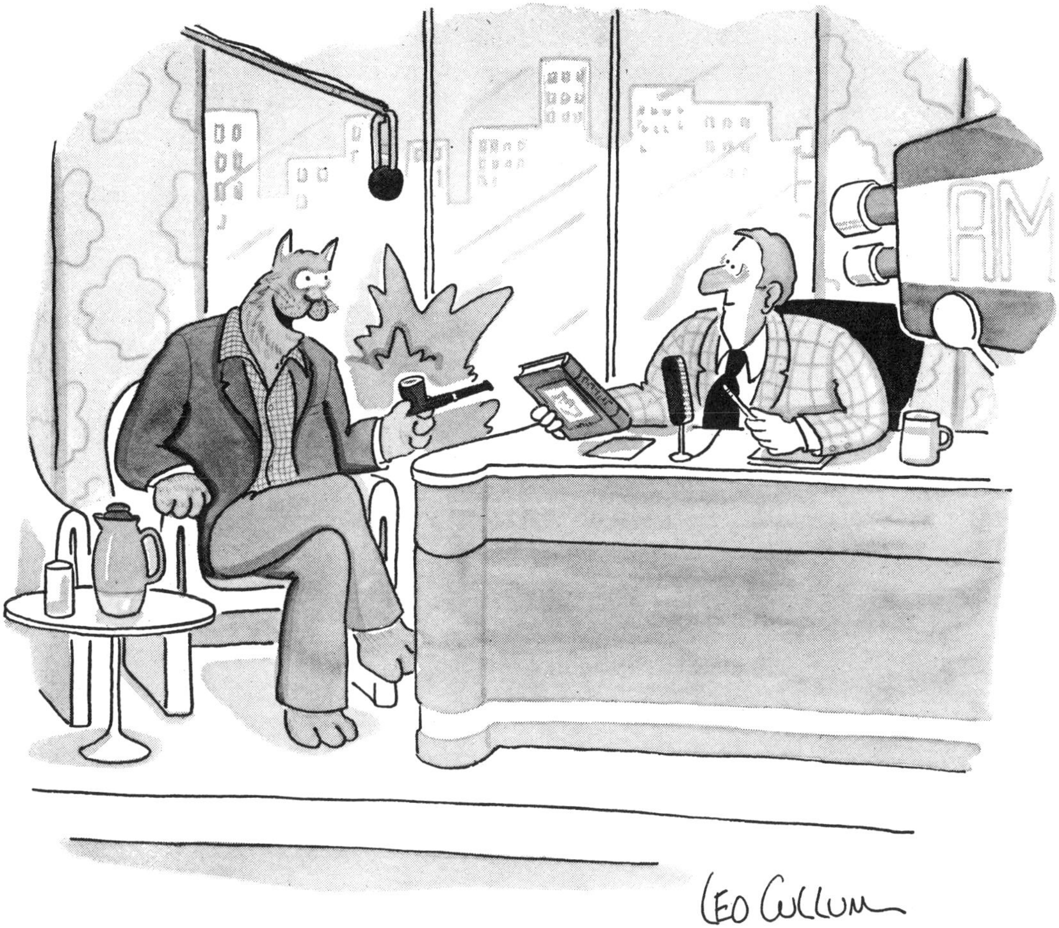
AM
LEO CULLUM

"I know a lot of people will say 'Oh, no—
not another book about cats.'"

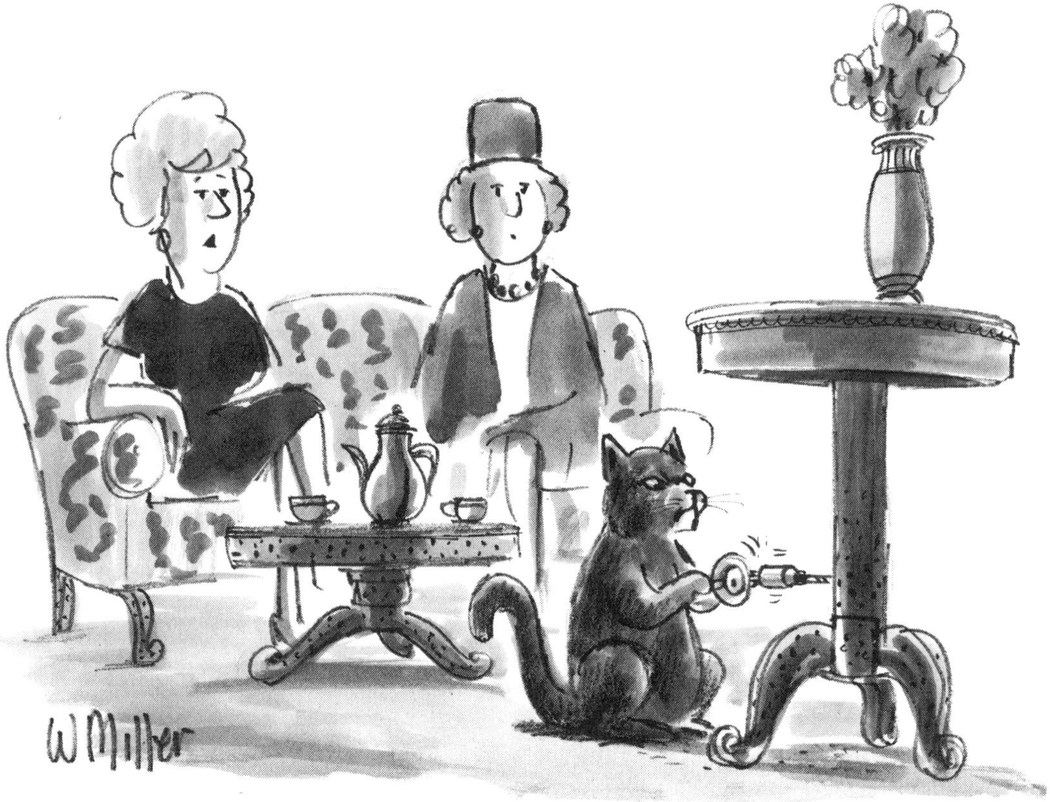
W Miller

"We had her declawed, but she's still impossible."

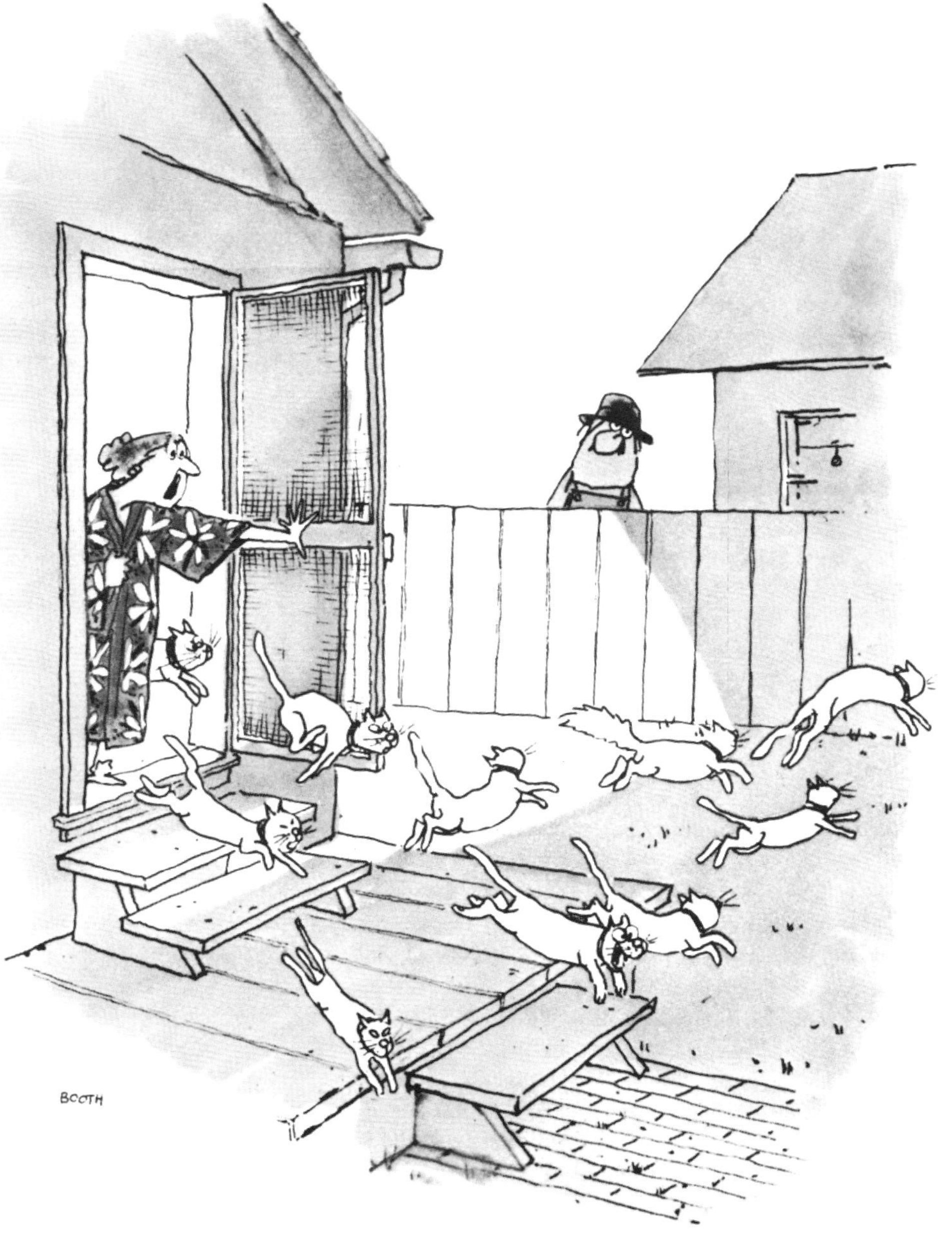
BOOTH

"Everyone be home by two o'clock!"

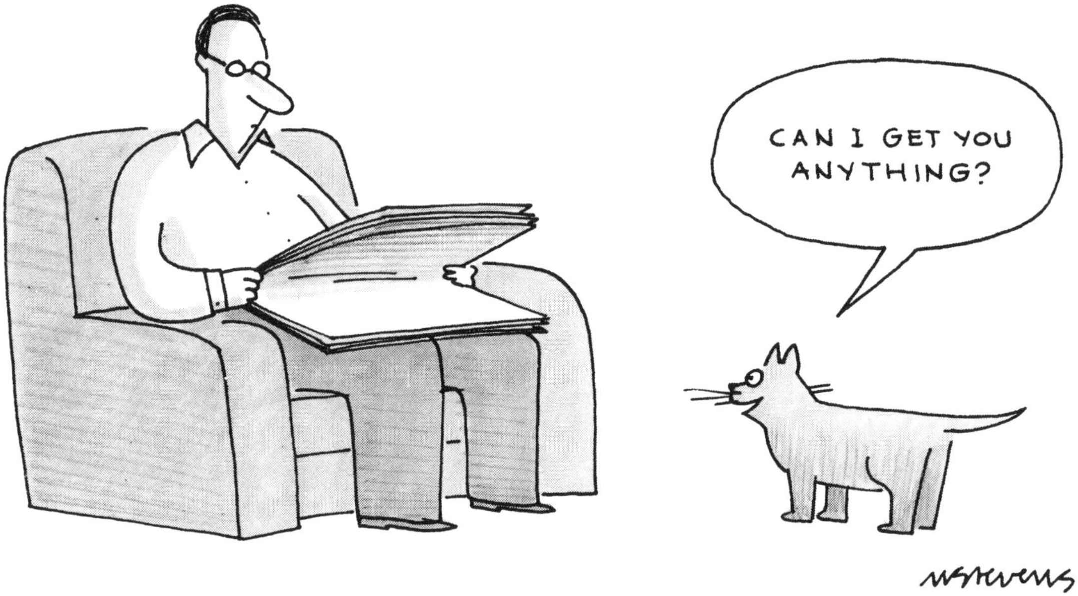
CAN I GET YOU ANYTHING?

NEW, IMPROVED CAT

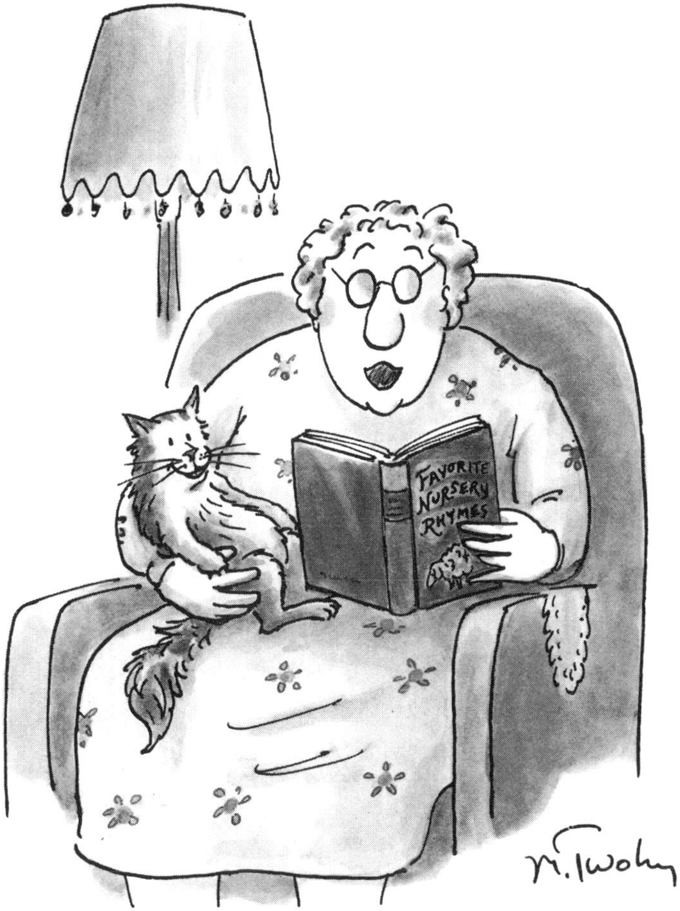
FAVORITE NURSERY RHYMES

"But when she got there, the cupboard was bare, and so the poor dog had none."

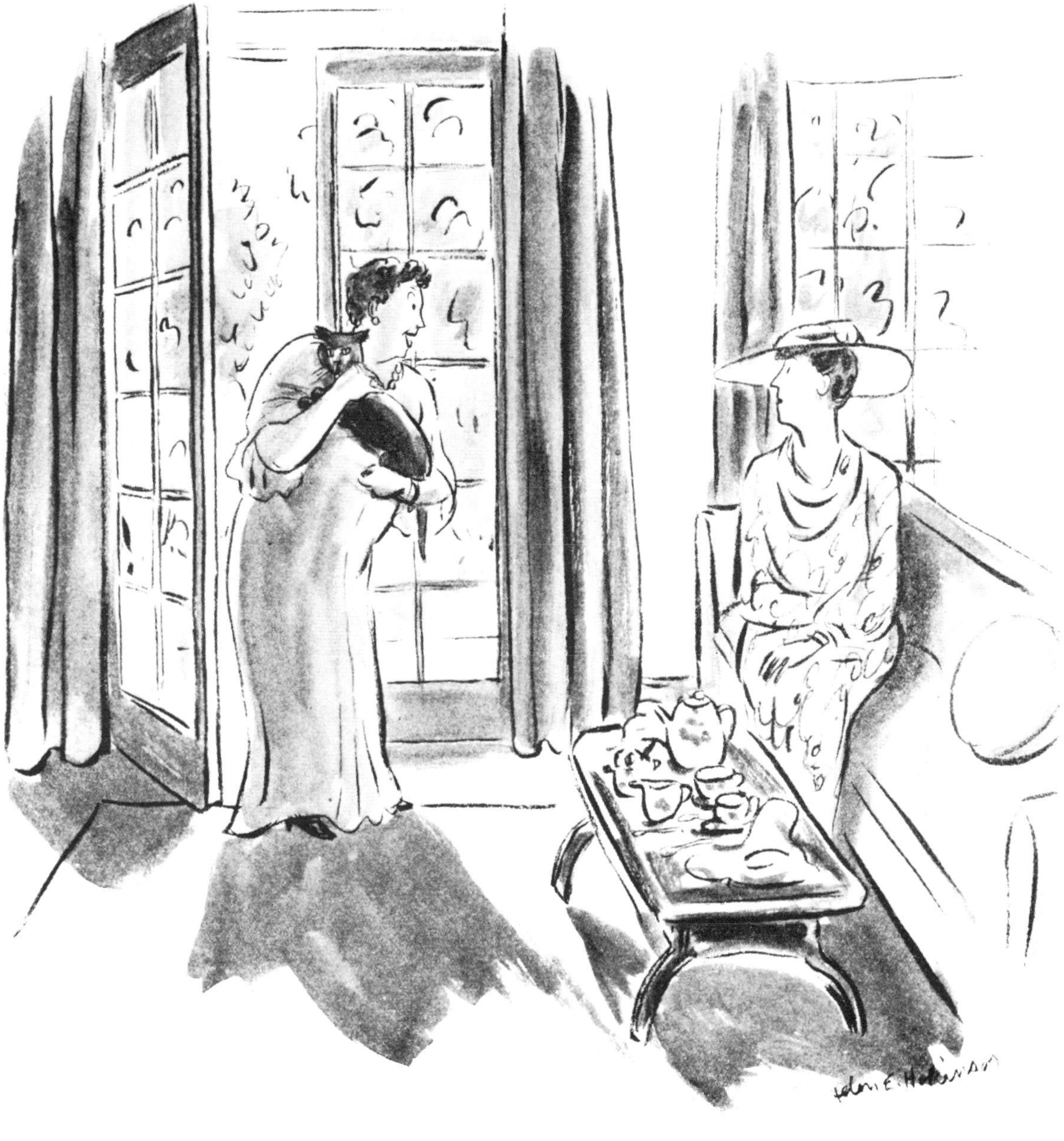

"Guess what we've done. We've just caught a mouse!"

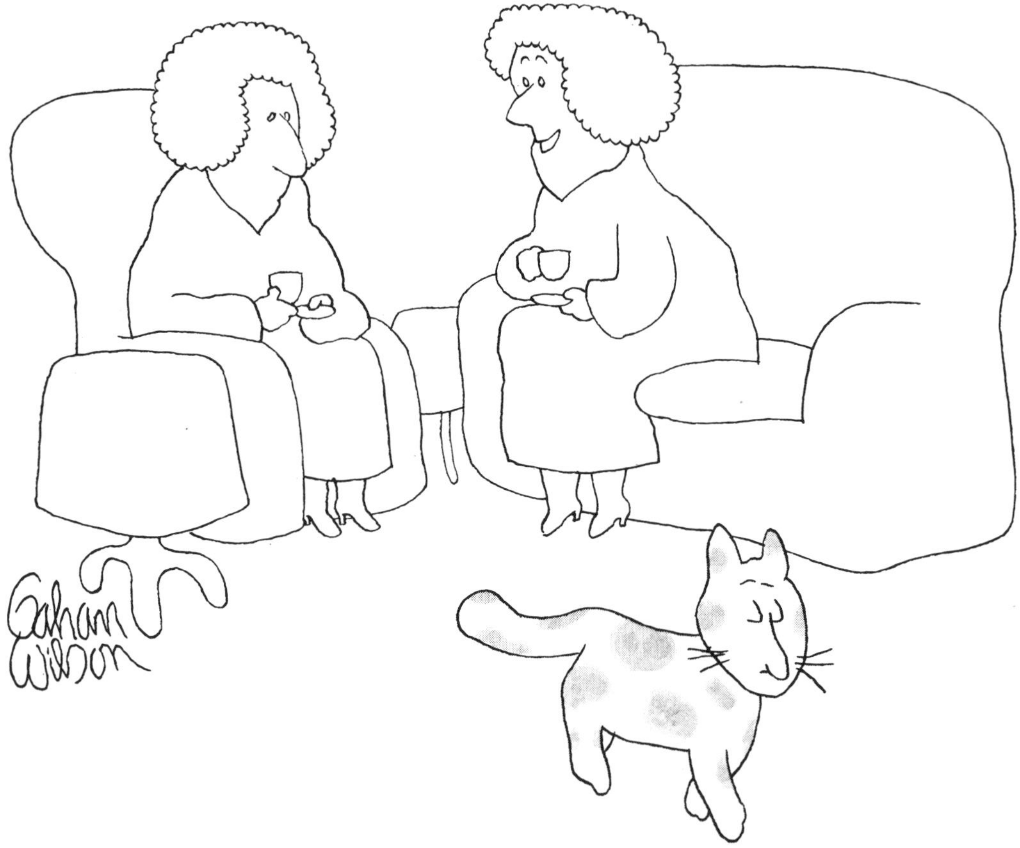
Gahan Wilson

"I've never seen him pause next to anyone longer!"

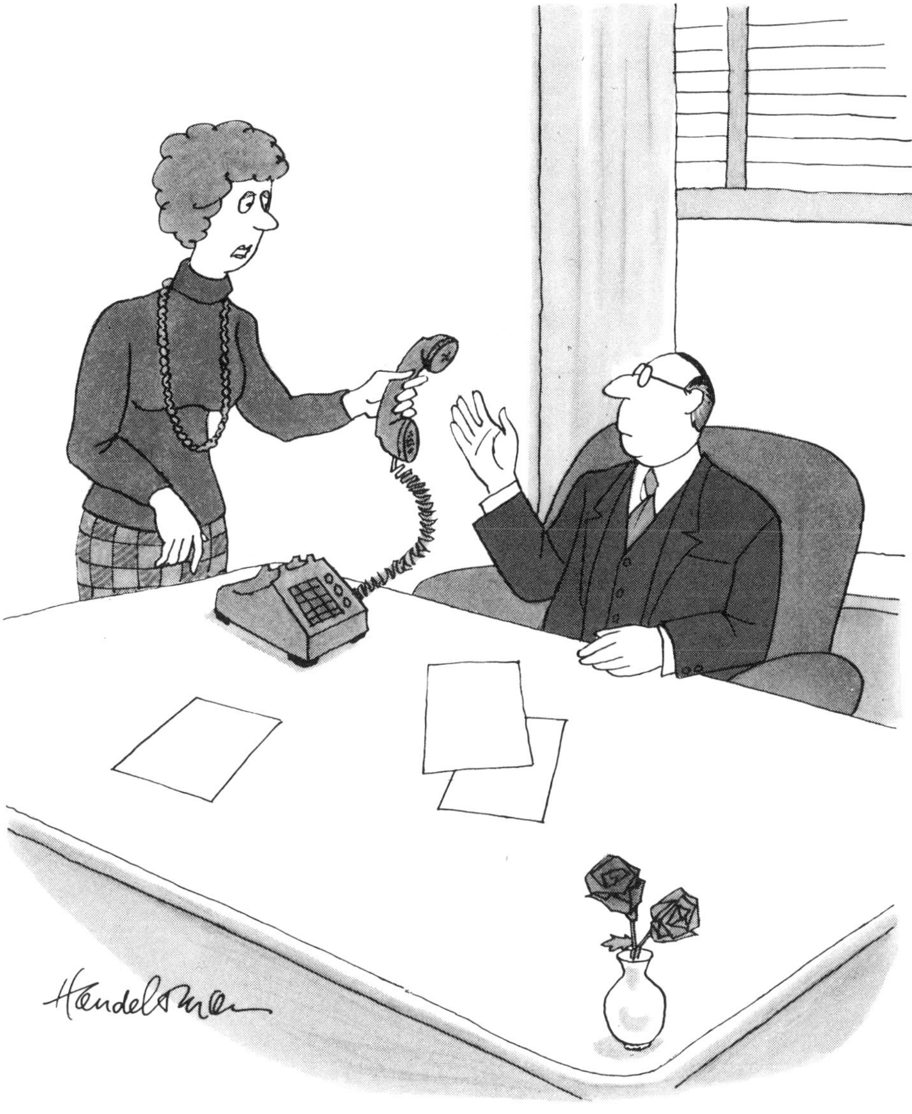
Handelsman

"Your wife feels that your cat needs to hear an authoritative male voice."

"Am I talking to __myself__?"

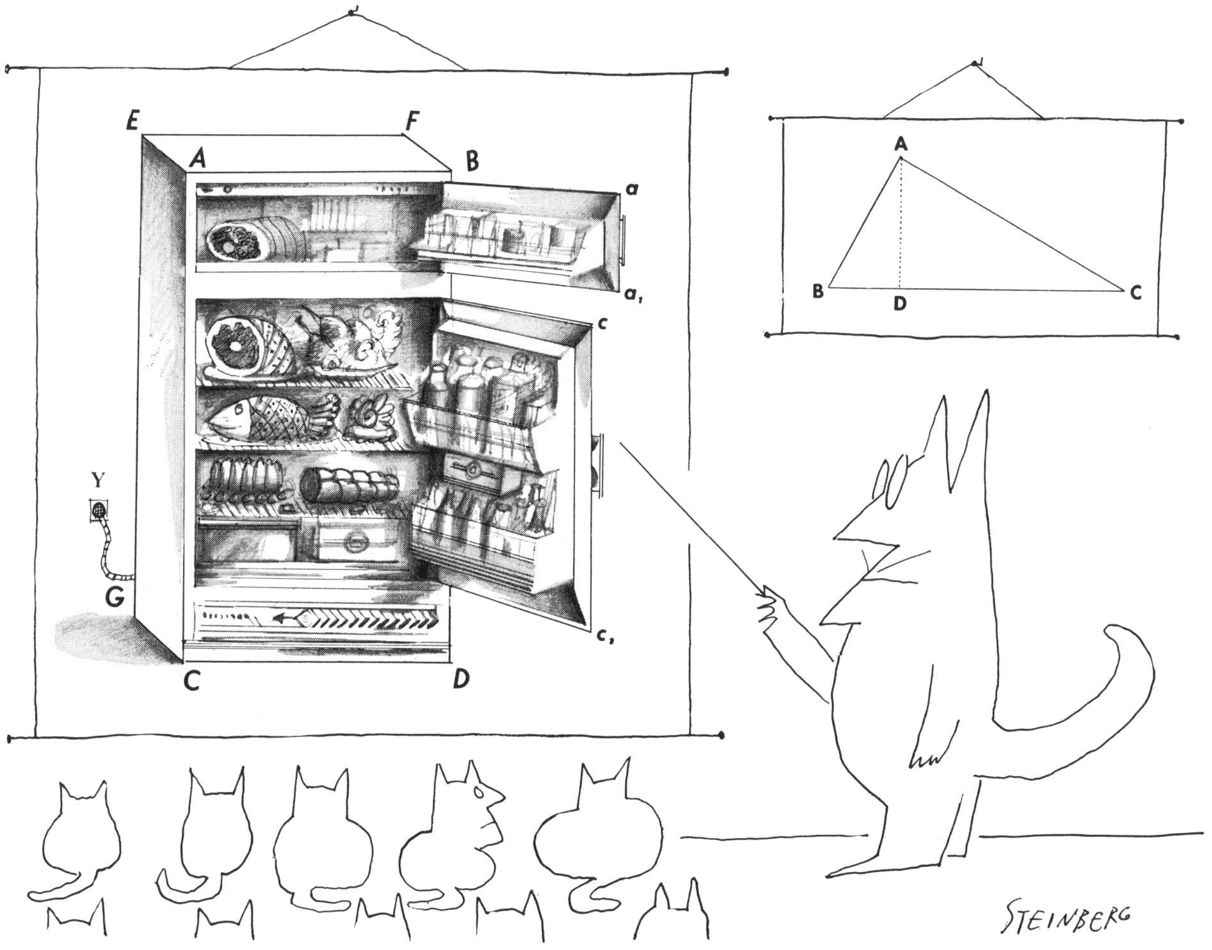
E
F
A
B
a
a,
c
Y
G
c,
C
D
A
B
D
C
STEINBERG

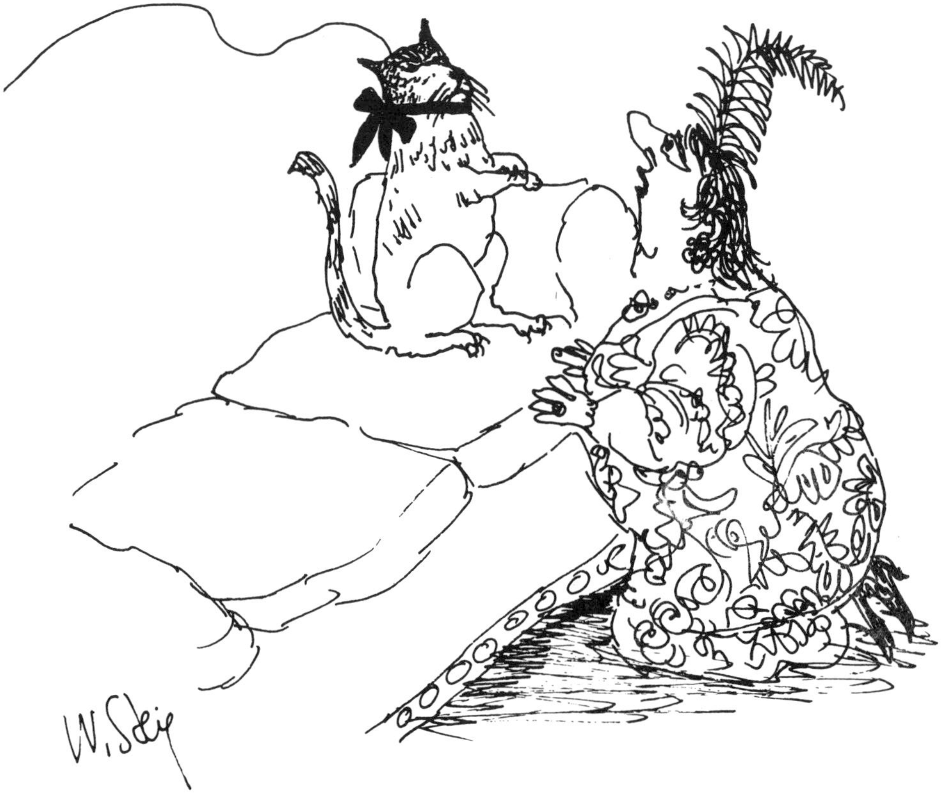
W. Steig

"All right, darling, I promise. No more canned food."

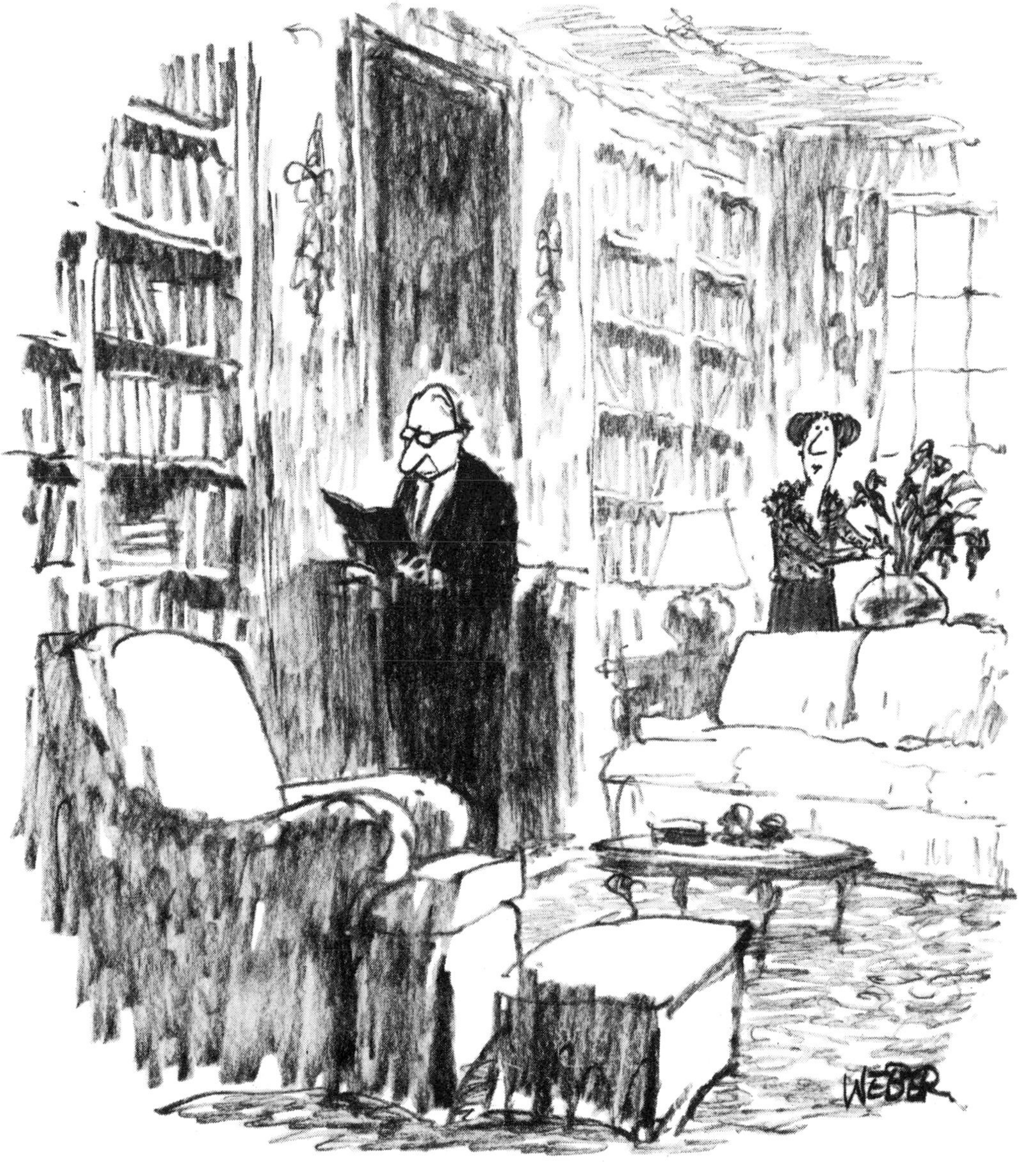
WEBER

"By the way, I've ordered a cat."

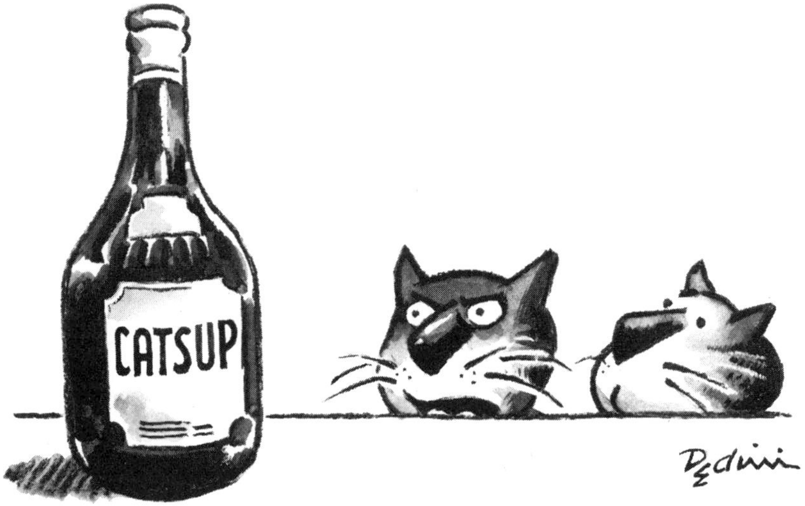
CATSUP

"Makes you wonder, doesn't it?"

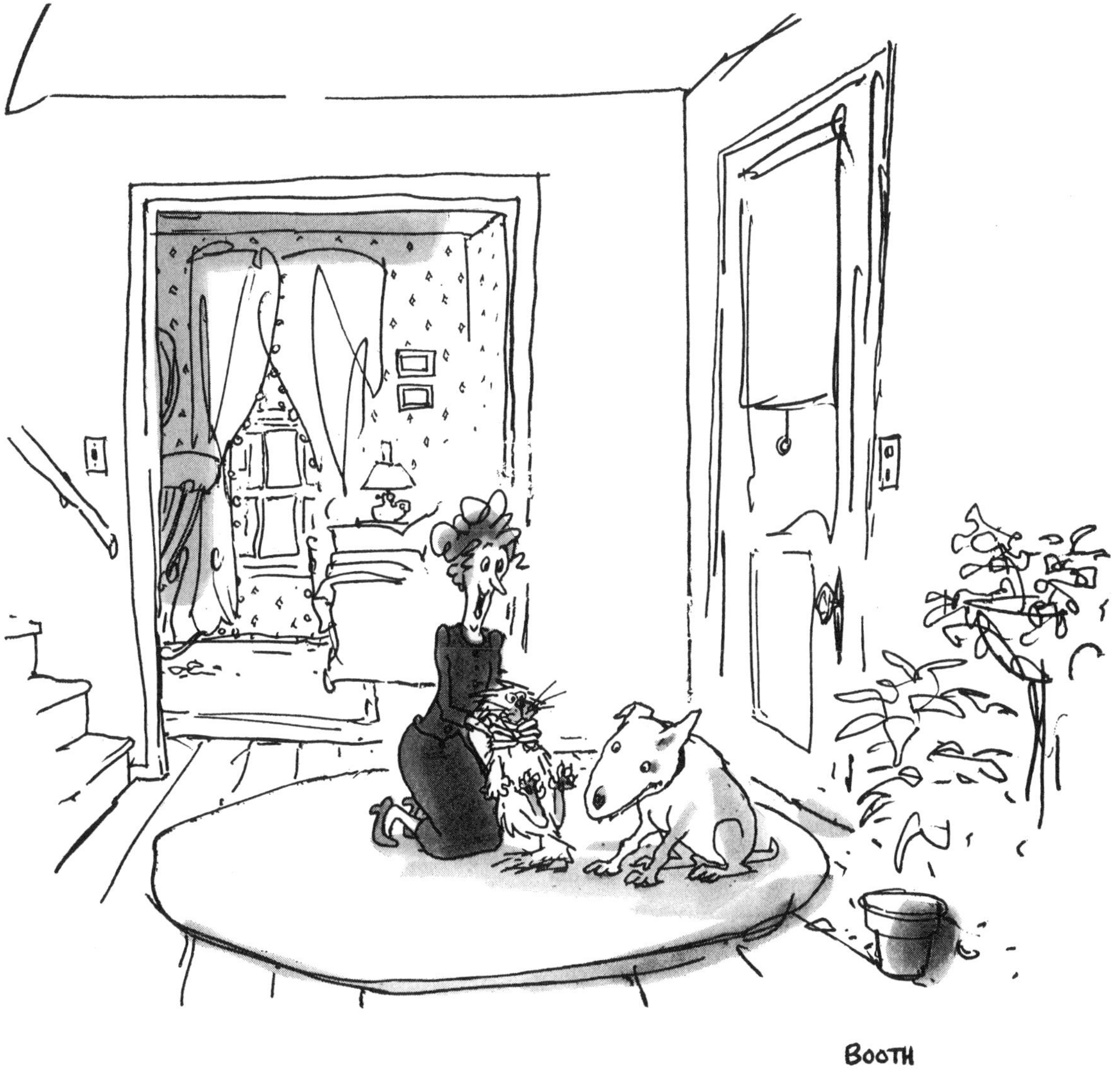
BOOTH

"From this day forward, we will do our very best to do unto Pussy as we would have Pussy do unto us."

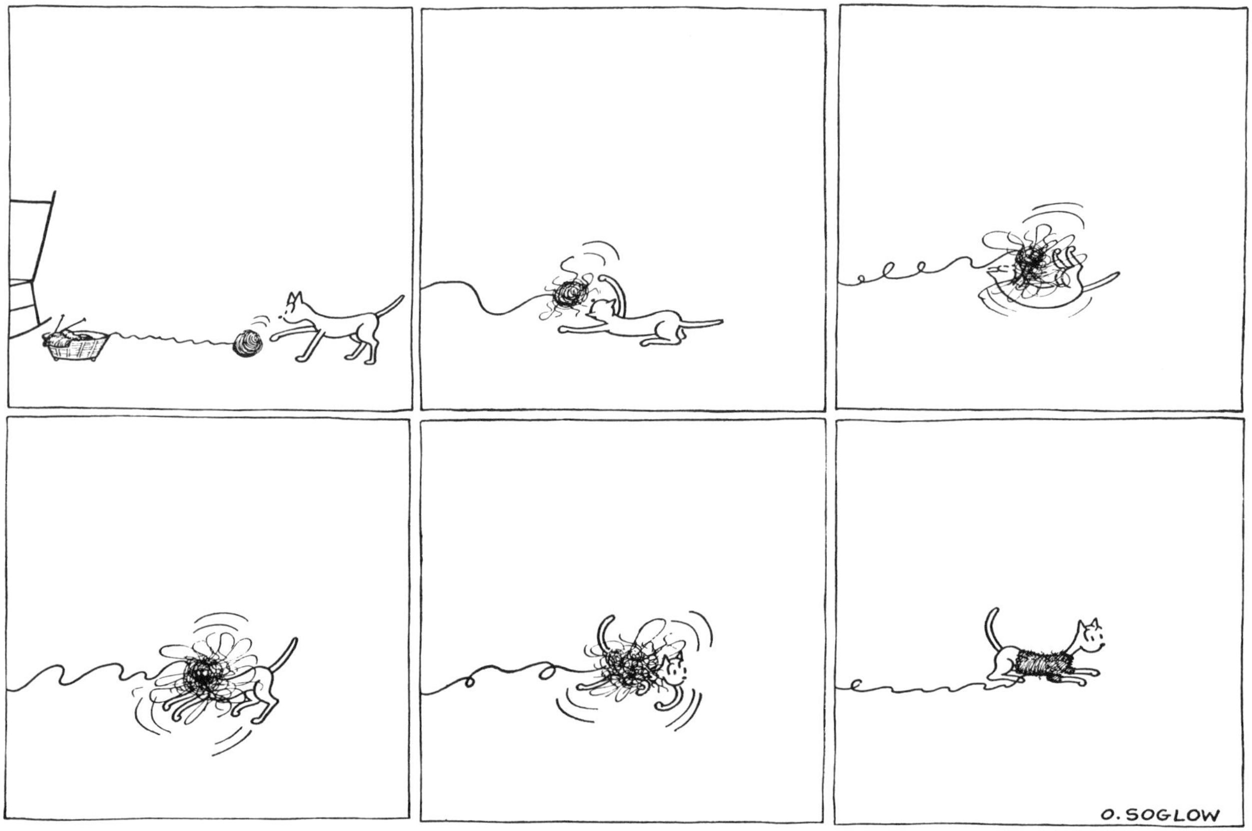
O. SOGLOW

"This year I'm just going to give everybody kittens."

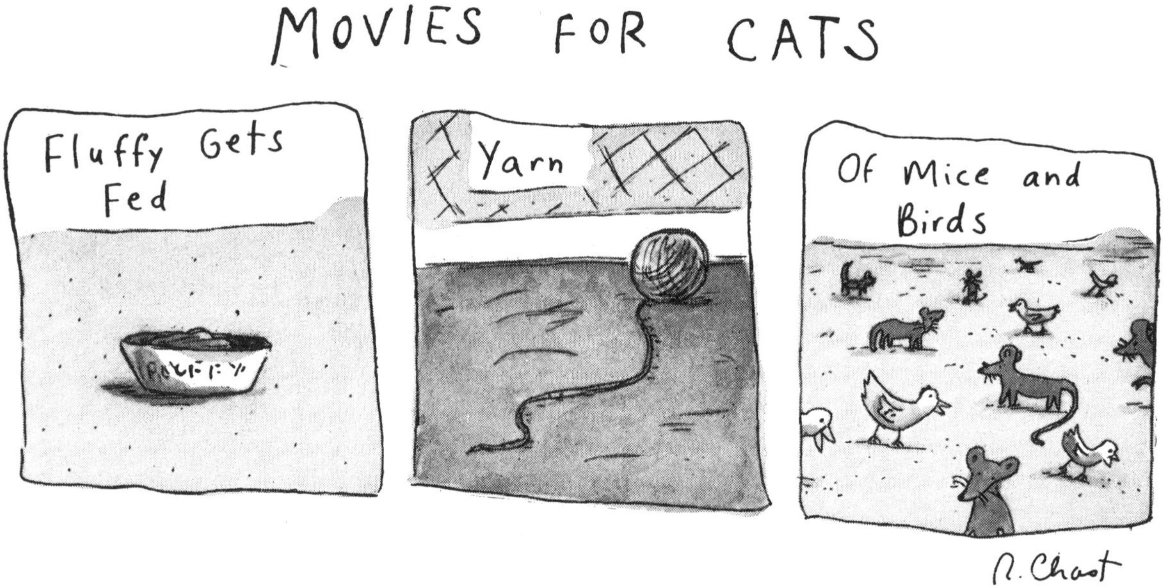
MOVIES FOR CATS
Fluffy Gets Fed
Yarn
Of Mice and Birds
R. Chast

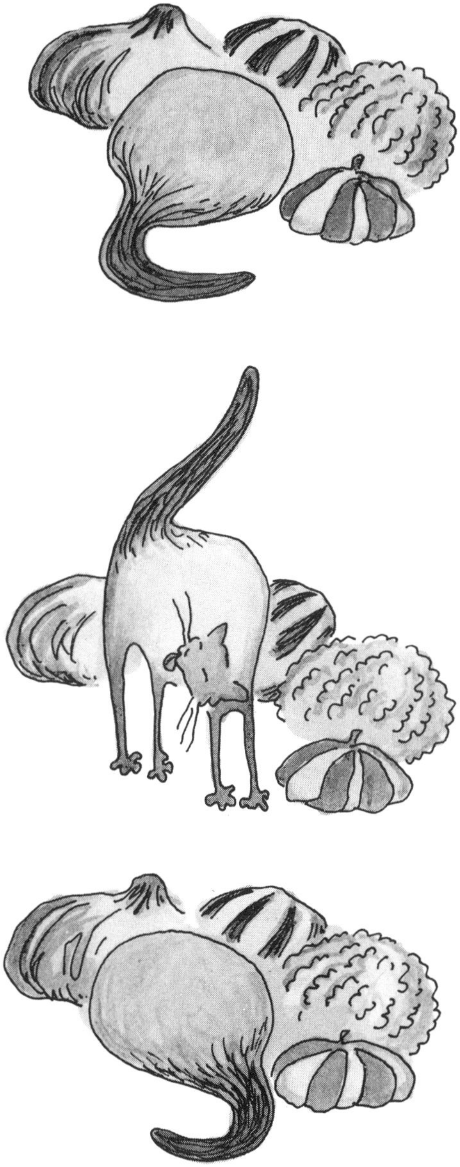
Shanahan

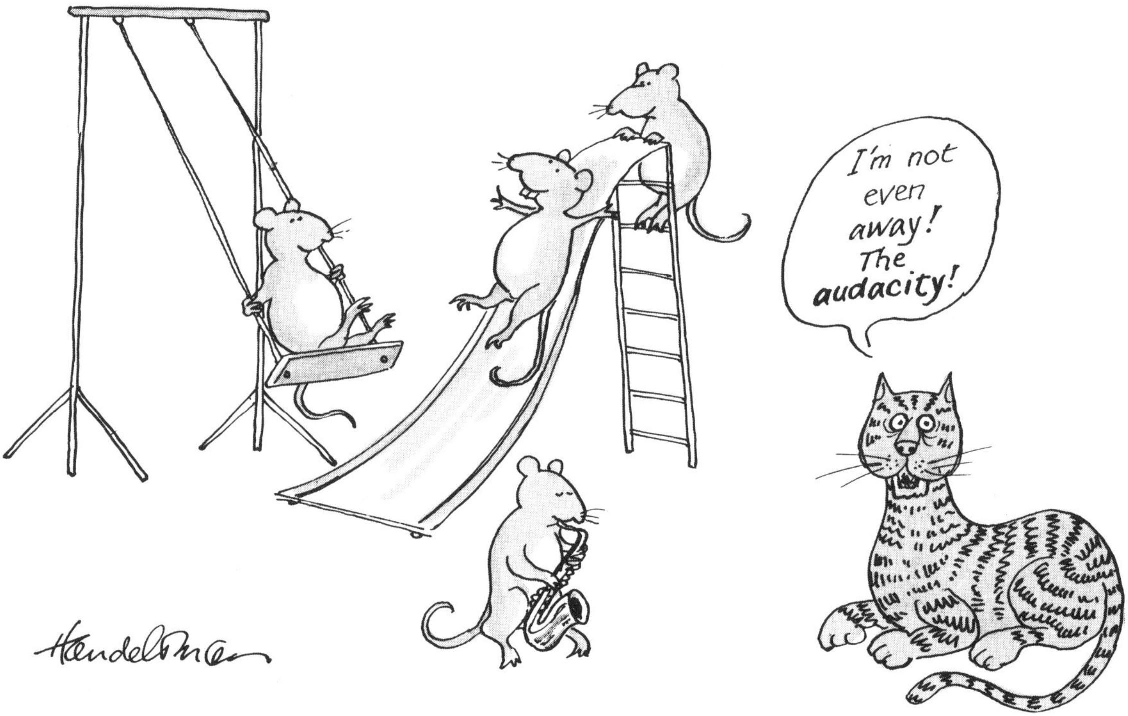
I'm not even away! The audacity!

"One final question: Do you now own or have you ever owned a fur coat?"

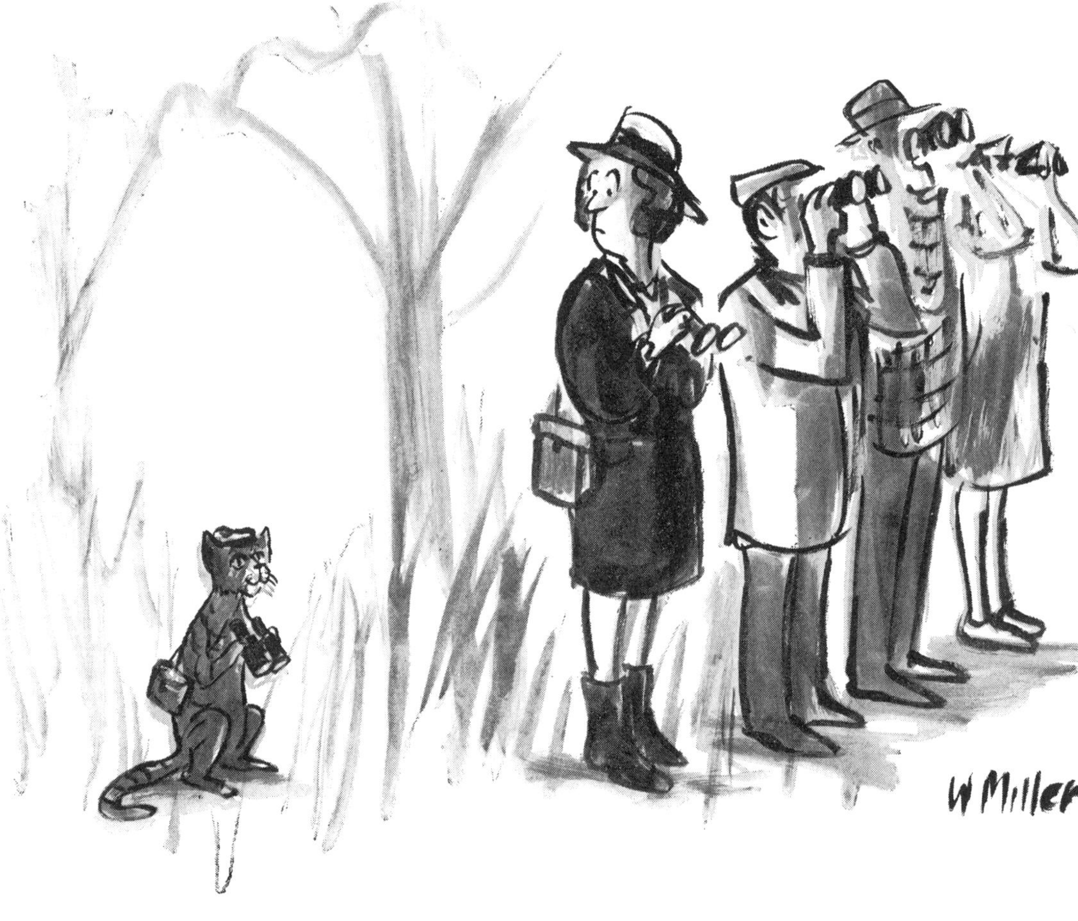
W Miller

ST.

ACT TAC ATC TCA CTA

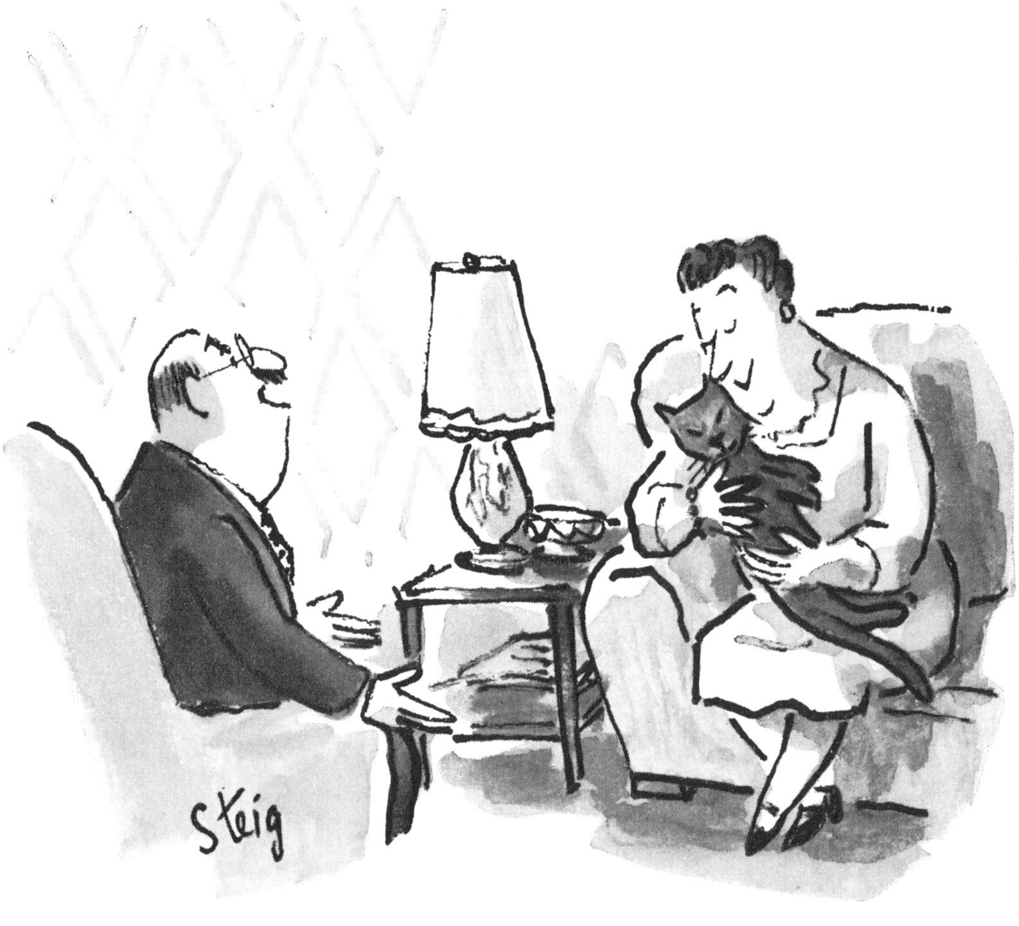
Steig

"It's very simple. If I was a cat, you would love me."

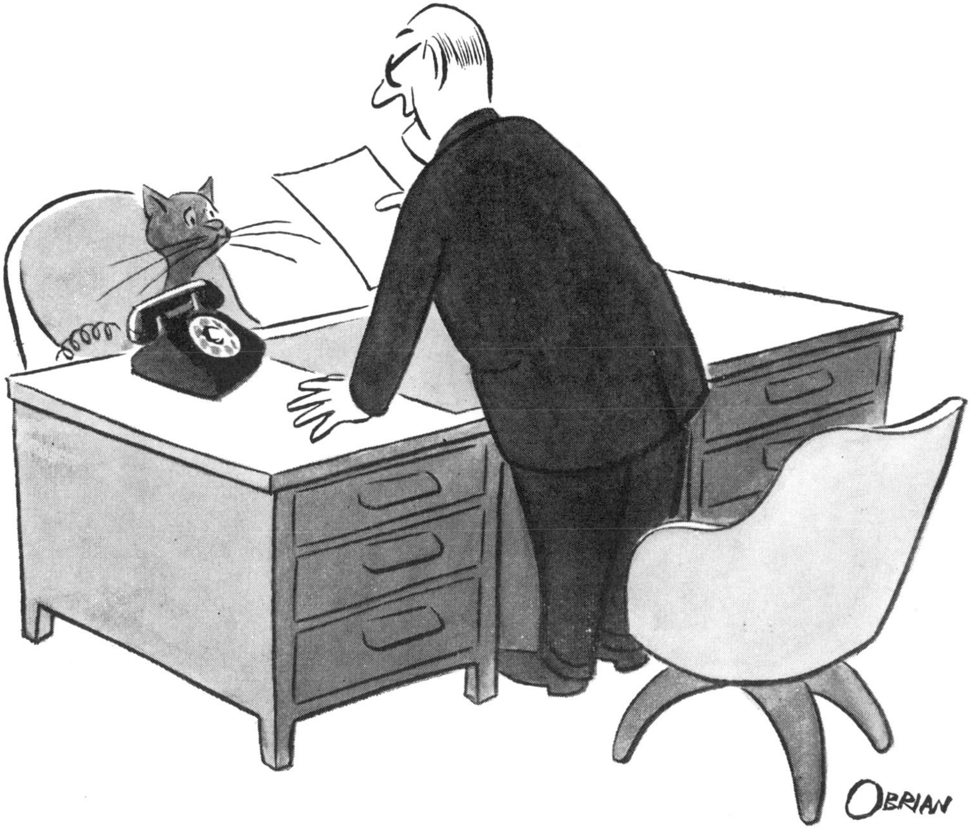
OBRIAN

"Before reading Miss Simpkins' will, may I say that you are a very lucky cat?"

"Margo, I think it's time we talked about us."

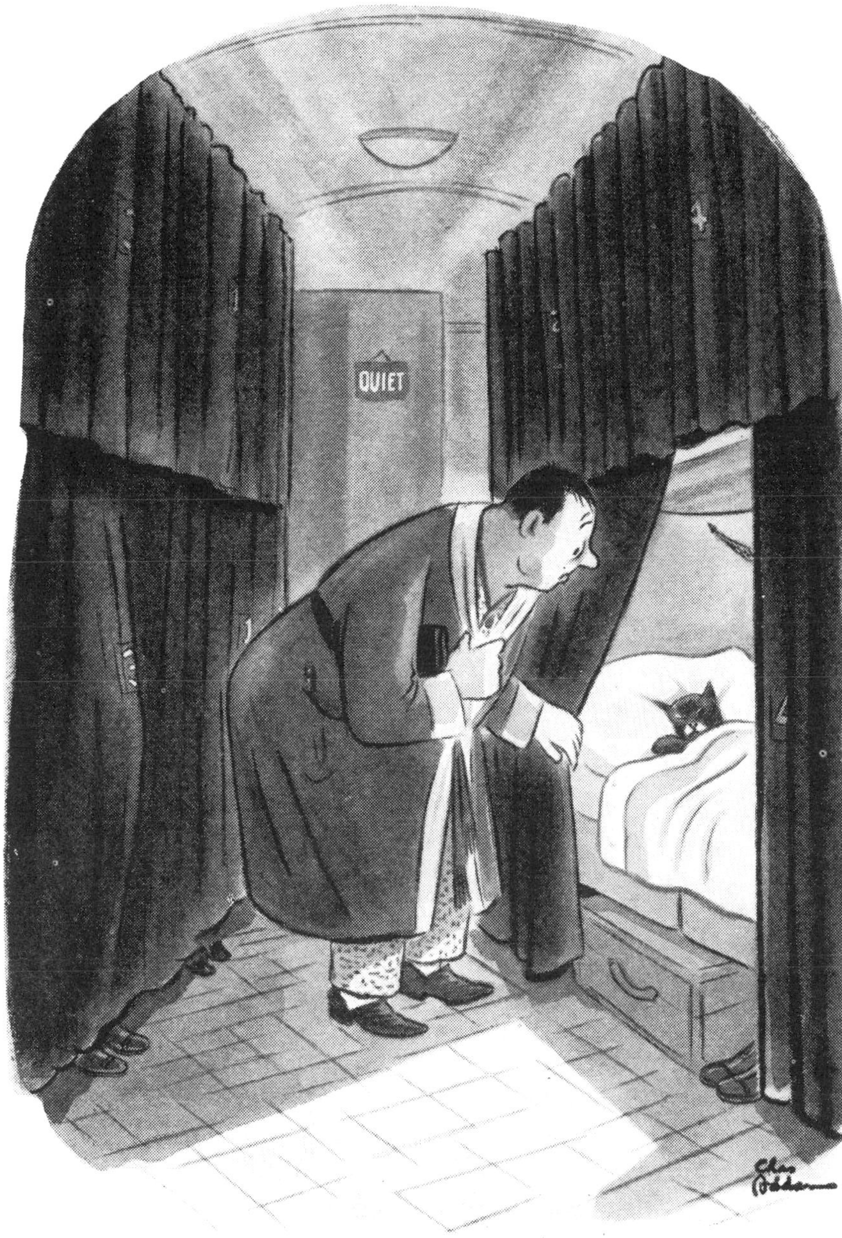
QUIET

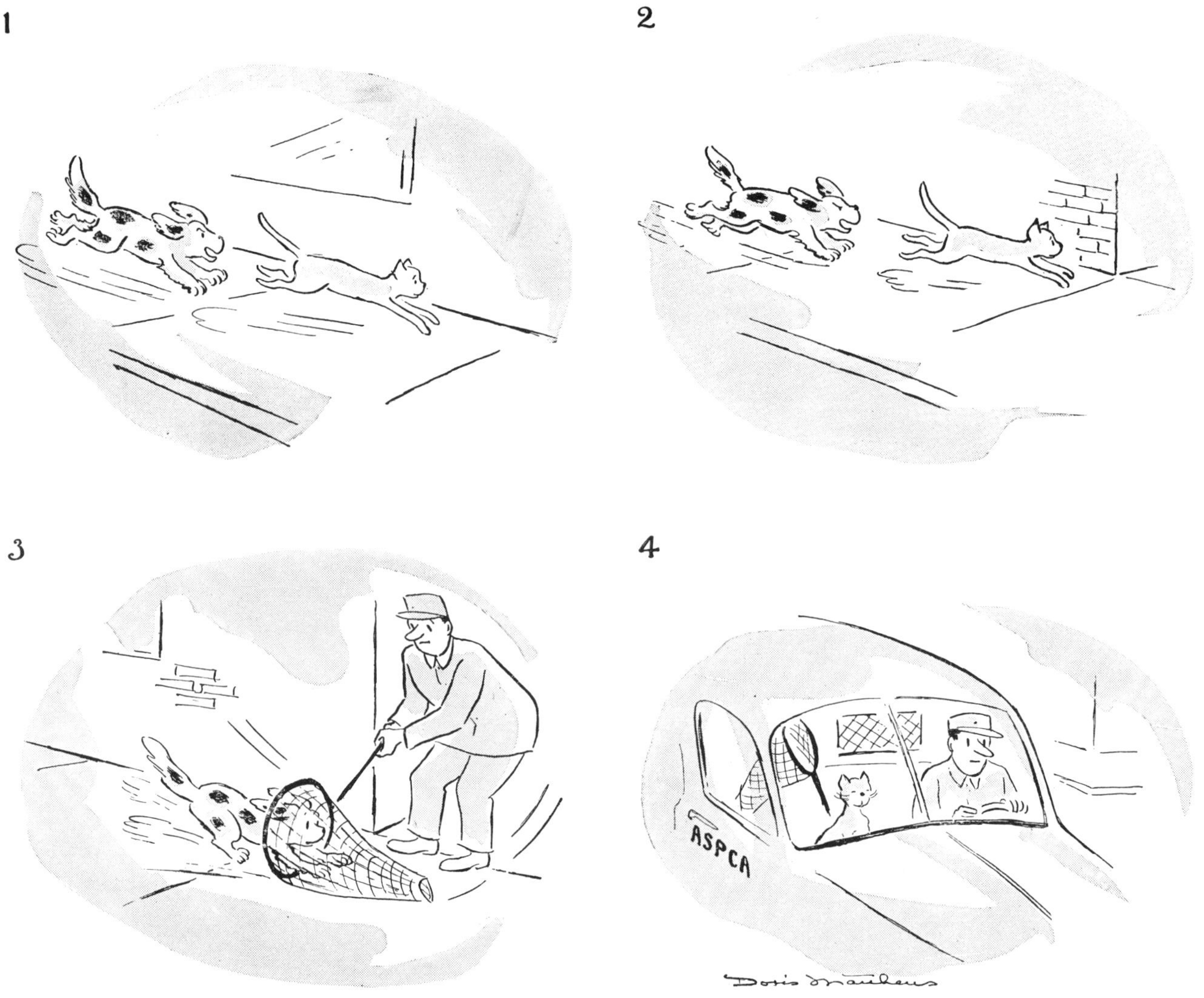
1
2
3
4
ASPCA

"When she was little, we had a very close relationship,
but now we're just friends."

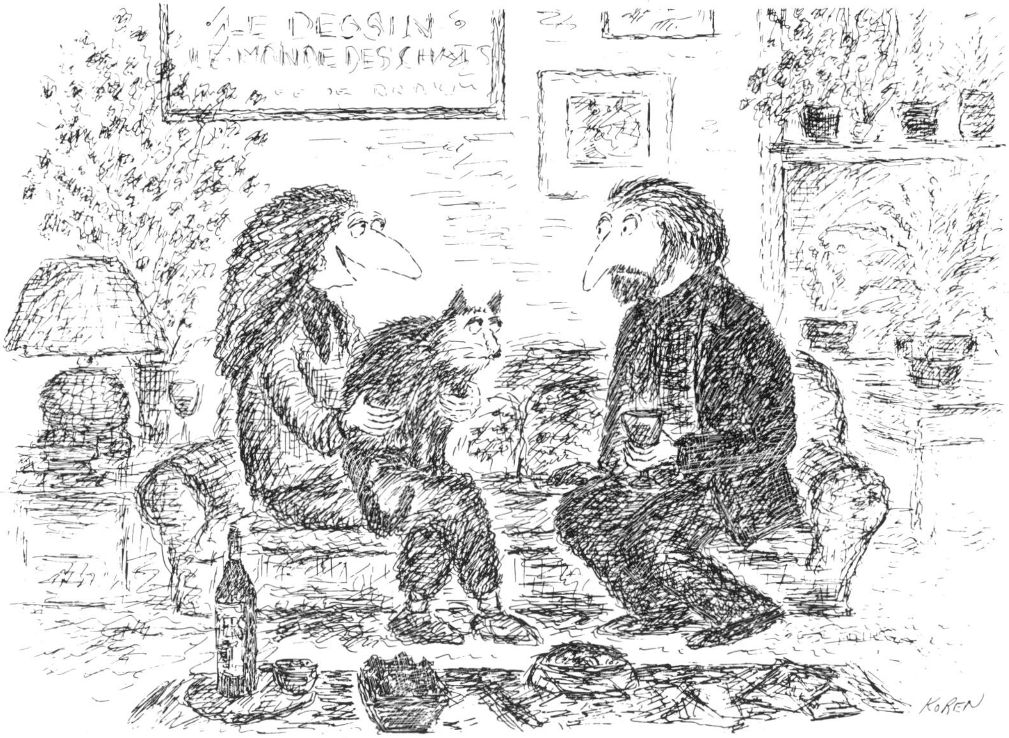
LE DESSIN
LE MONDE DES CHATS
KOREN

"Around here his word is law."

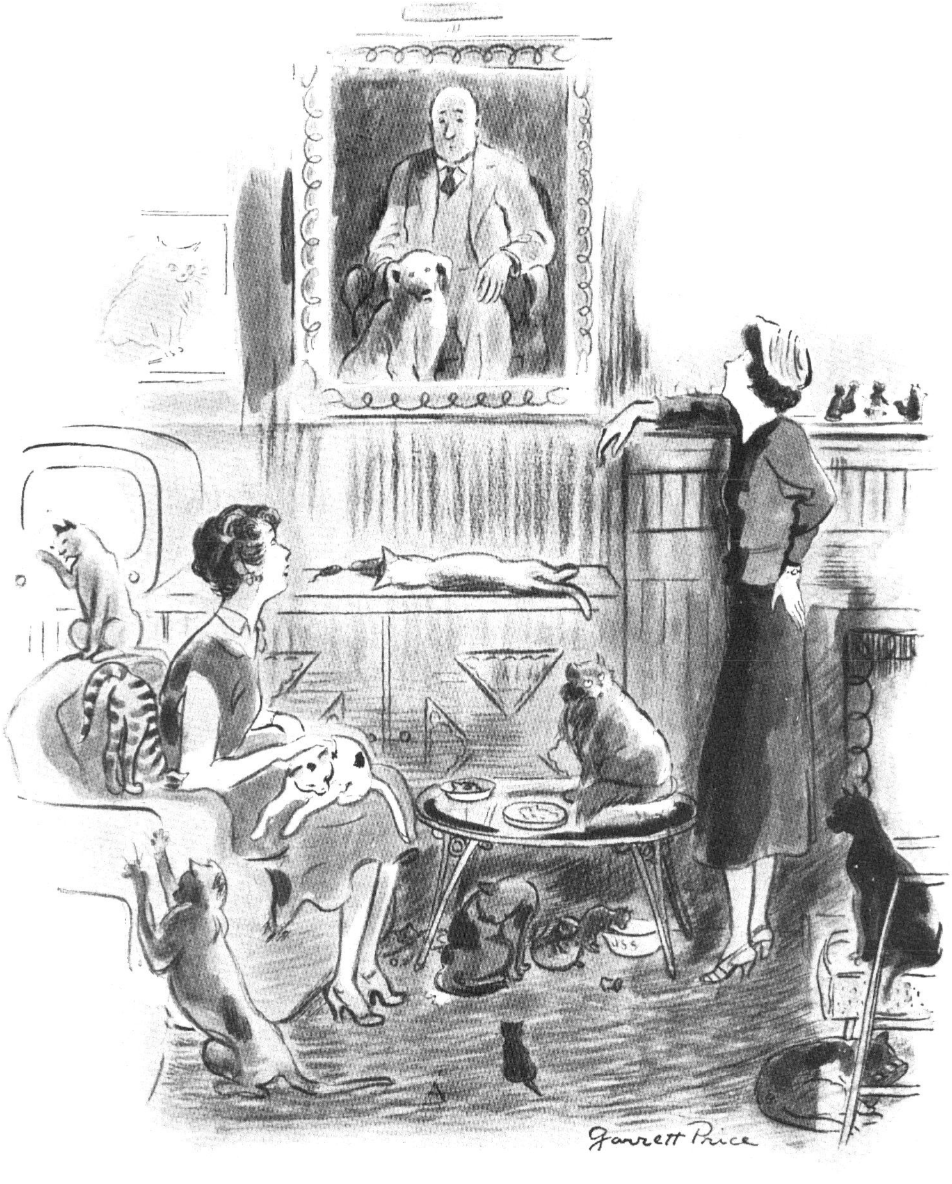
Garrett Price

"One morning they went out for a walk, and that's the last I ever saw of them."

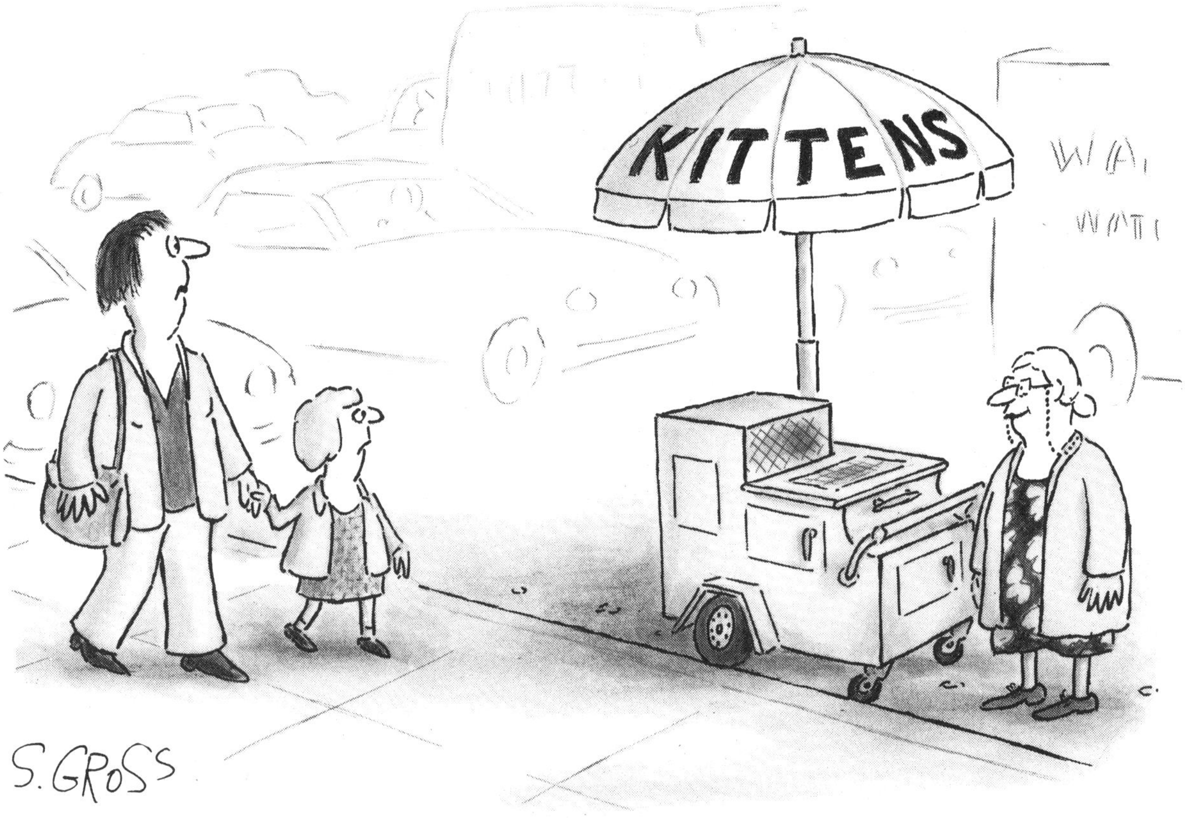
KITTENS
S. GROSS

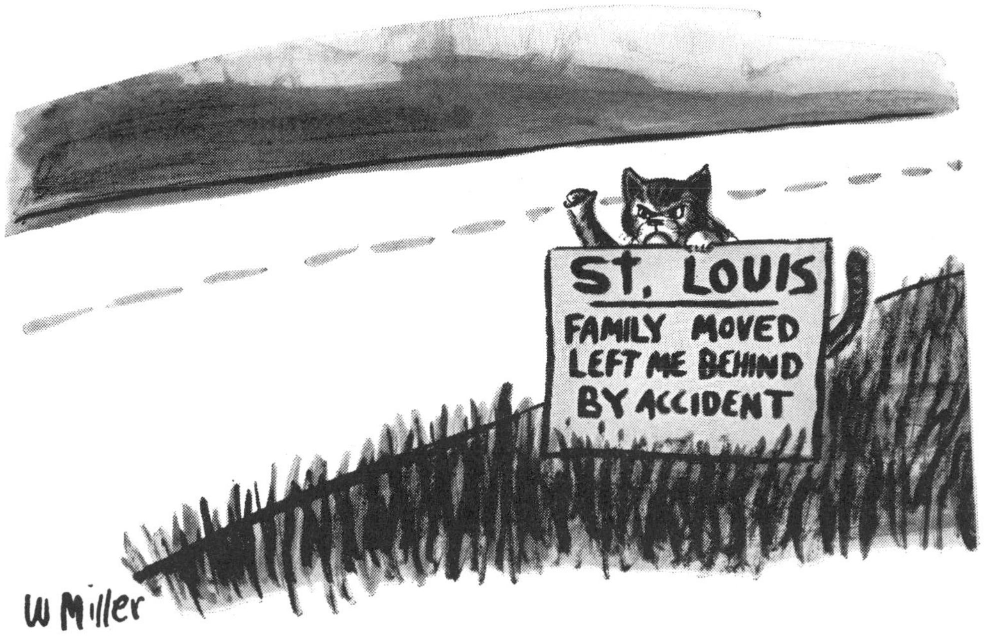
ST. LOUIS
FAMILY MOVED
LEFT ME BEHIND
BY ACCIDENT
W Miller

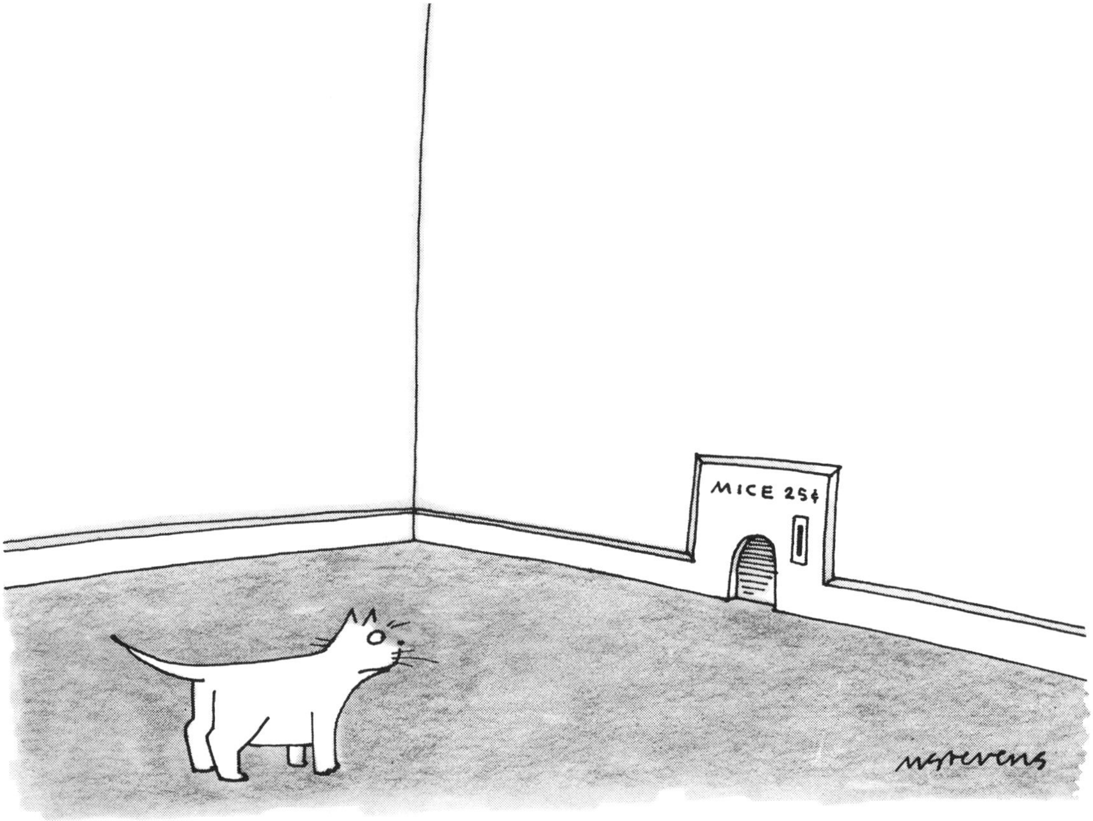
MICE 25¢
mstevens

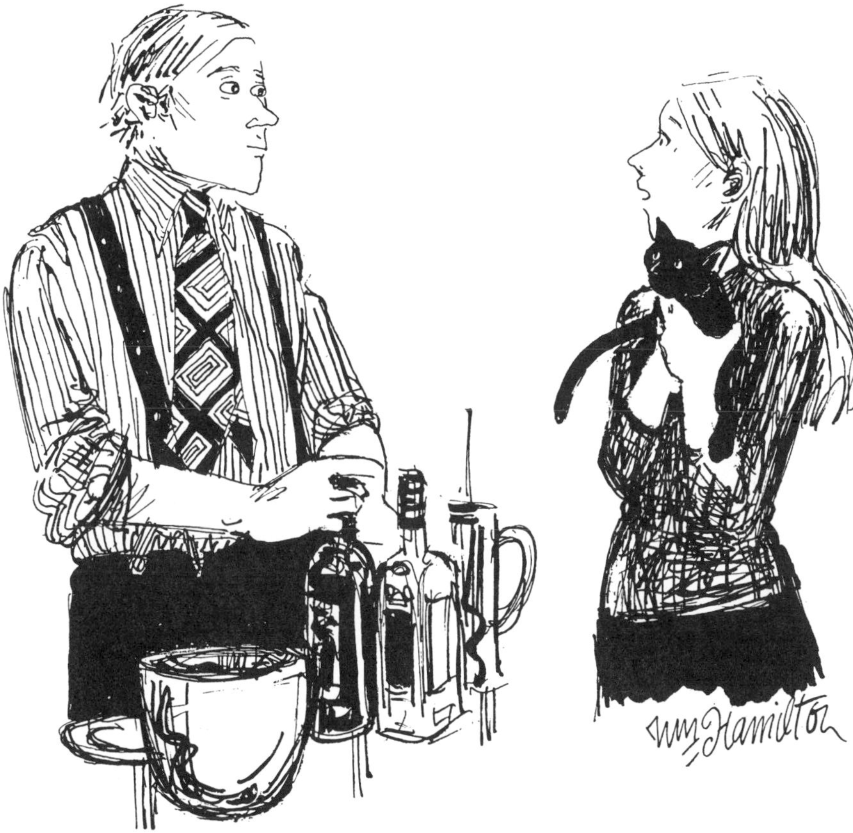
Wm Hamilton

"I mean, God, Philip, what if he doesn't really <u>like</u> Tabby Treat but is only eating it so we'll feel less guilty?"

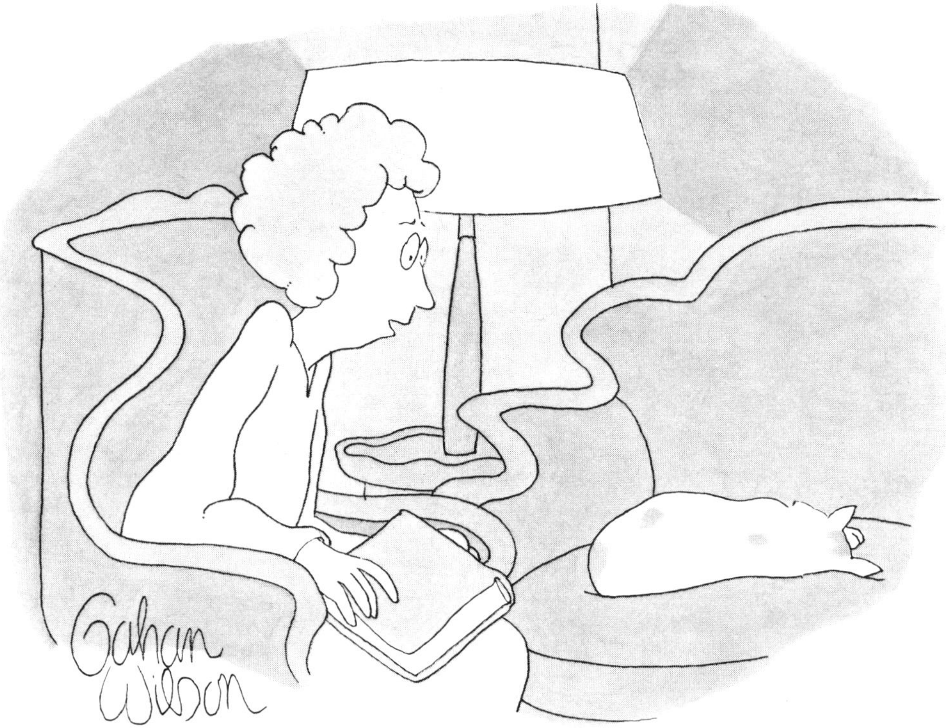
Gahan Wilson

"Are you all right?"

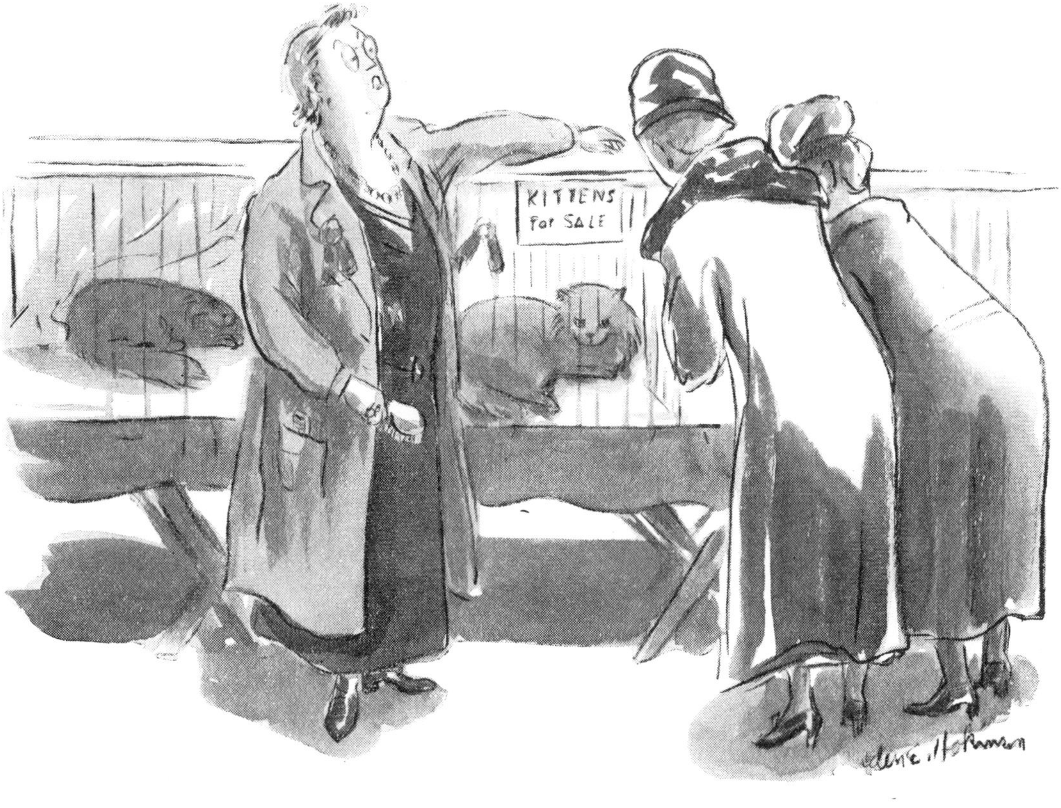
KITTENS
for SALE

*"Of course some cats have eight kittens
but I never have more than six."*

"We laugh at the same things."

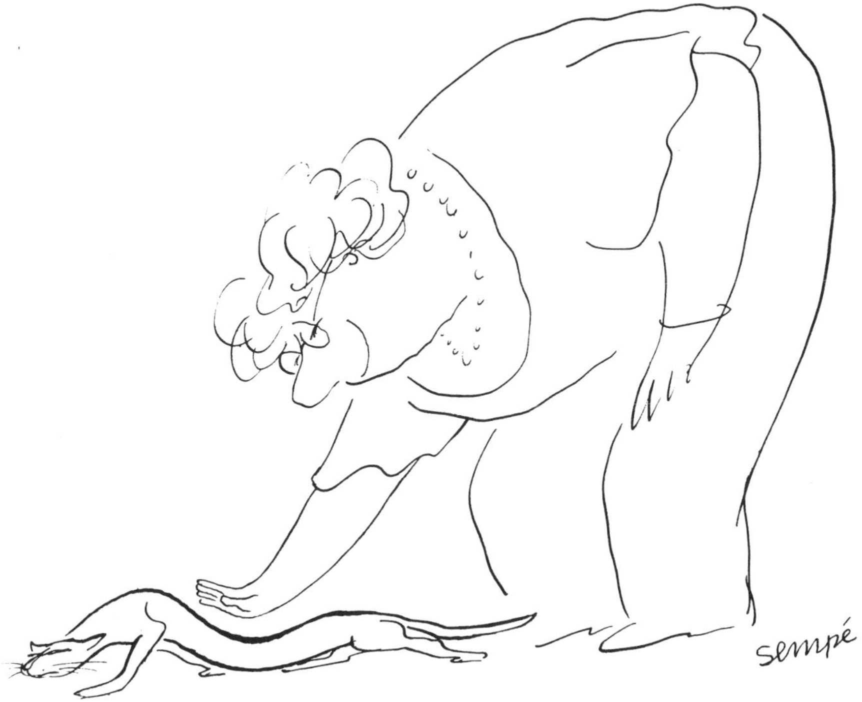
sempé

"Mrs. Wallace _made_ me take them. She said
they were as much ours as theirs."

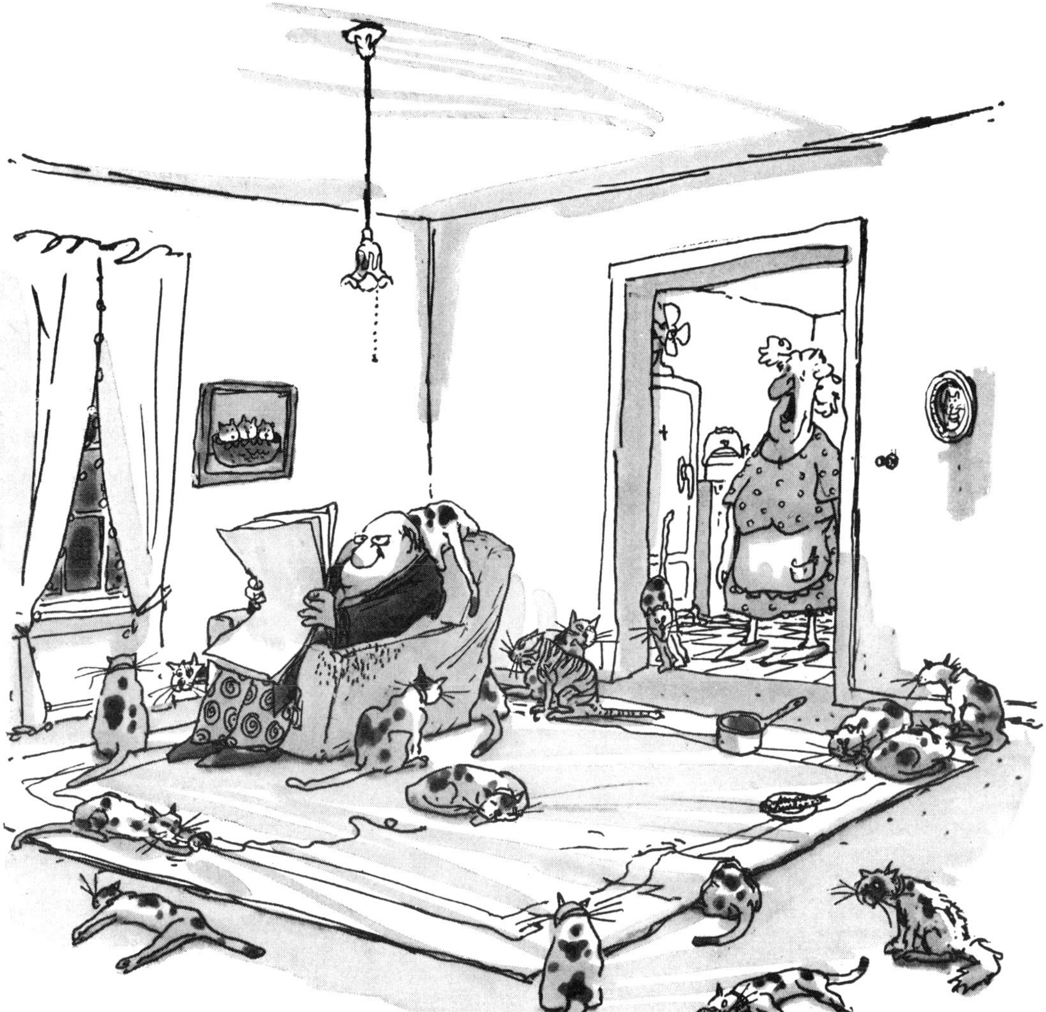
BOOTH

"Edgar, please run down to the shopping center right away, and get some milk and cat food. Don't get canned tuna, or chicken, or liver, or any of those awful combinations. Shop around and get a surprise. The pussies like surprises."

THE VIGIL

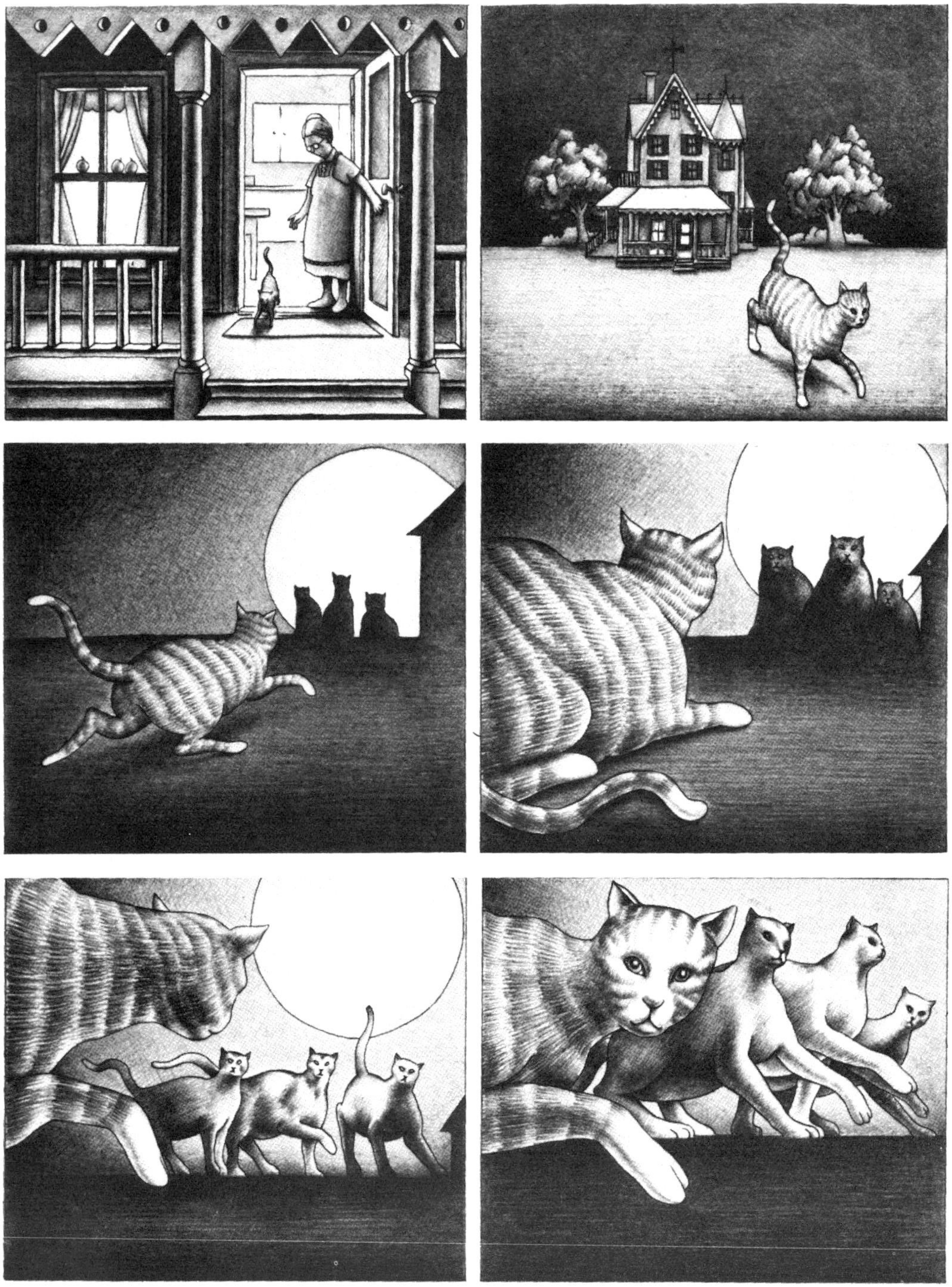

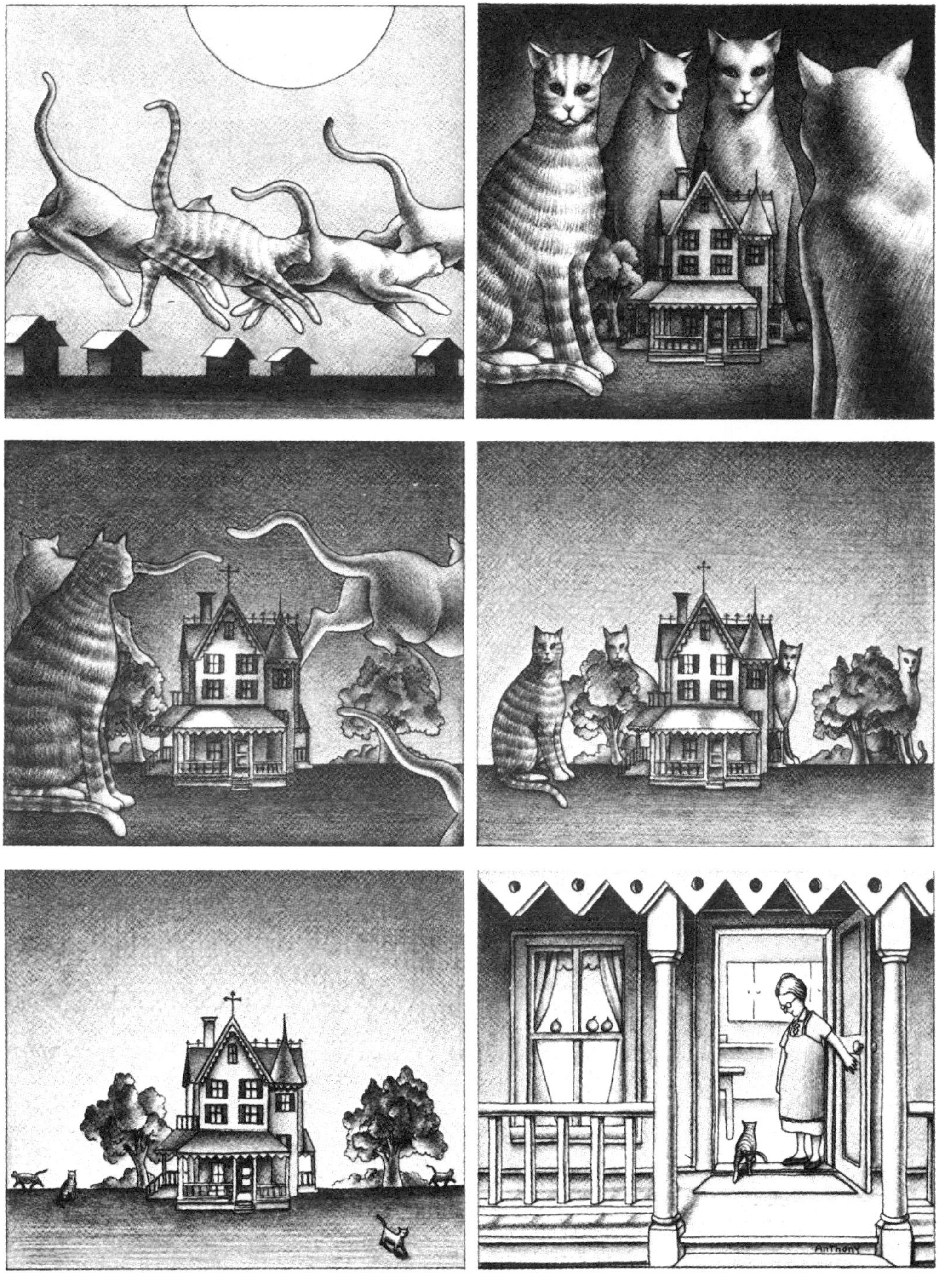
ANTHONY

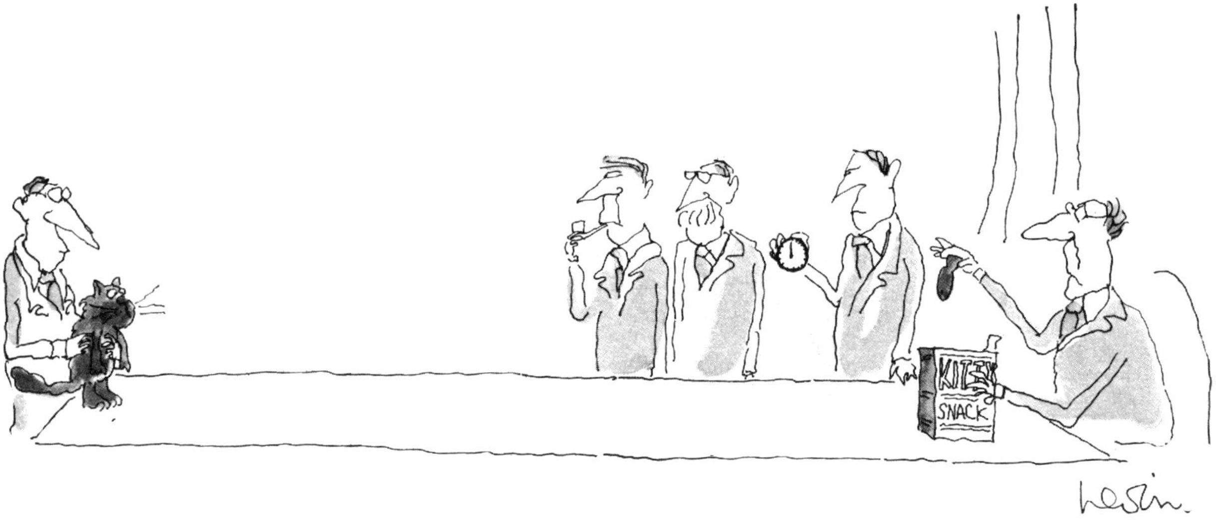
SNACK

Front row: Smarty, Itty Fitty, Daisy, Boo, Mercedes, Foo Foo, Aka.
Second row: Spanky, Charlie, Mouse, Tigger, KiKi, Fluffy, Honey, Jerry.
Third row: Sweetheart, Pumpkin, B.J., Dennis, Emlyn, Pearl, Annie.
Back row: Miss Perringer.

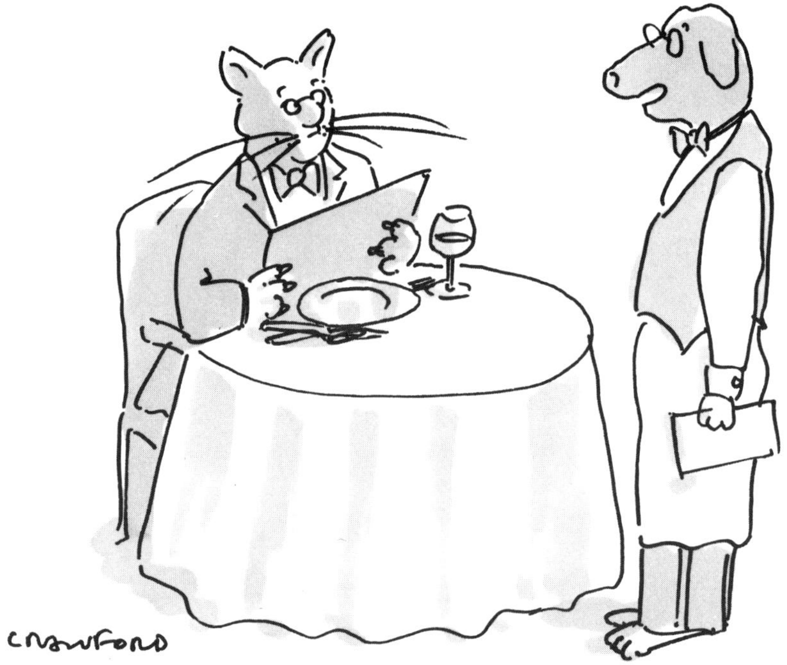
CRAWFORD

"We're out of the cat food. Permit me to recommend the dog food."

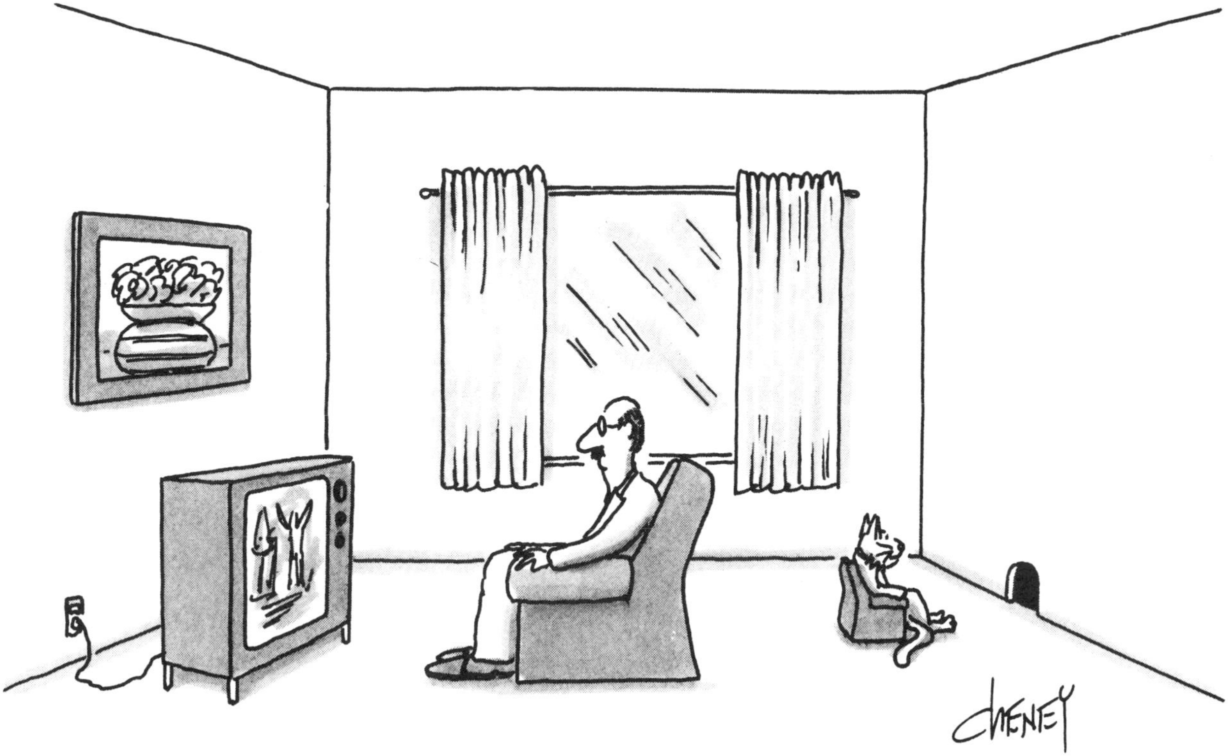
CHENEY

"*If I take too many naps during the day, I find it difficult to sleep well at night.*"

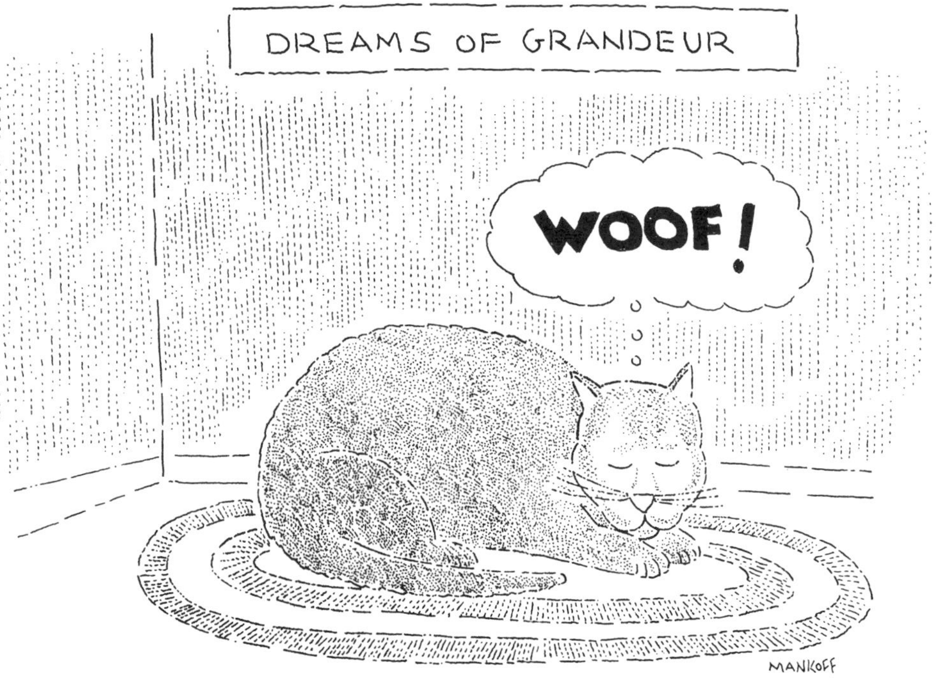
DREAMS OF GRANDEUR
WOOF!
MANKOFF

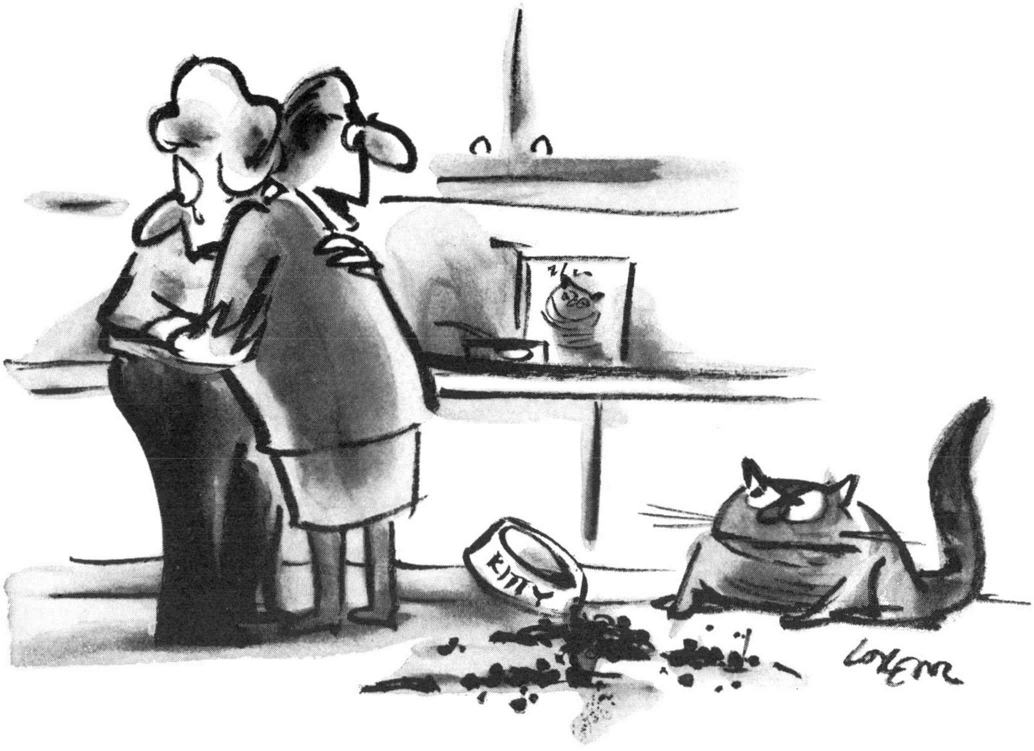
KITTY

"Well, I hope you're proud of yourself!"

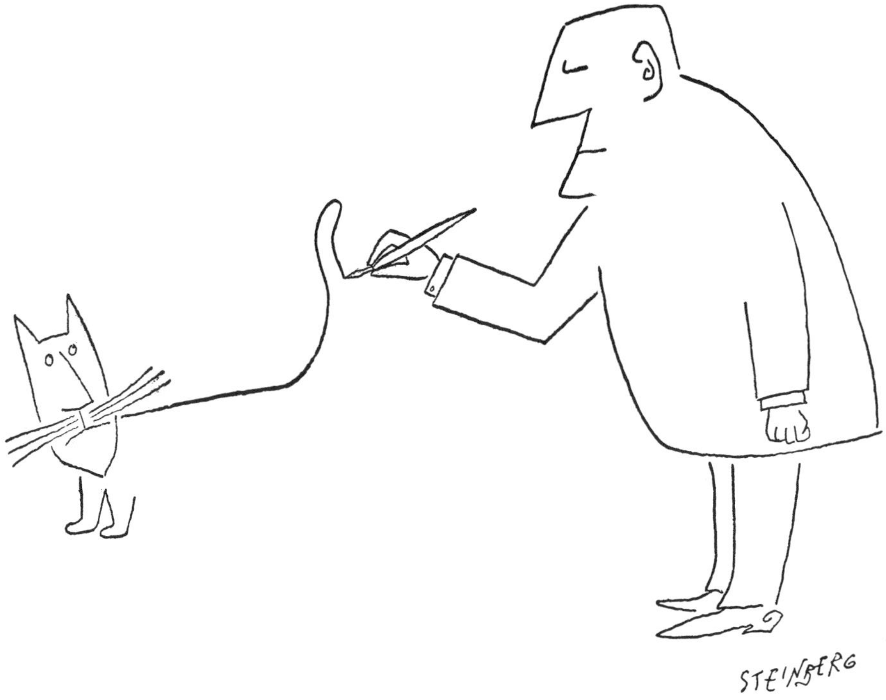
STEINBERG

BUDGIE DEFICIT

"*He knows I can't stand it when he doesn't eat.*"

"I've enjoyed our little talk, and now I'll have myself a nice little nap."

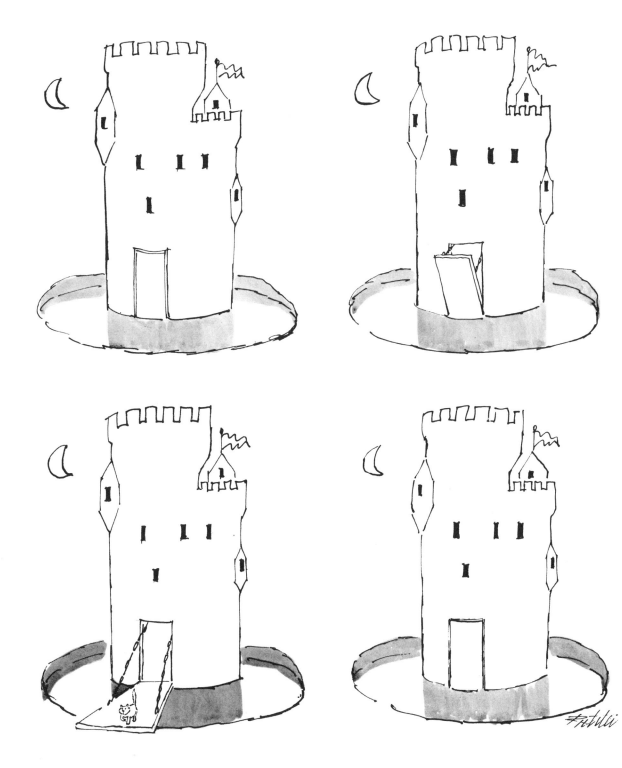

*"Like this—see? You've got to get
your back into it."*

"Is it all right for an expectant mother to catch chipmunks?"

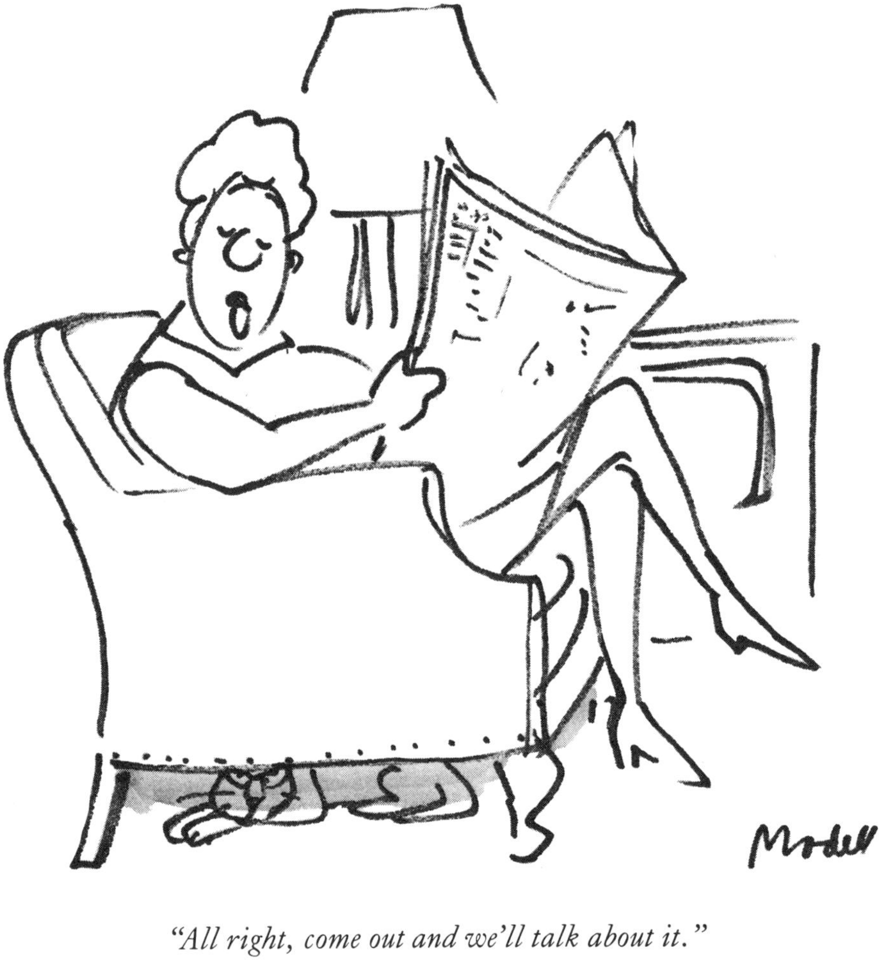
Modell

"All right, come out and we'll talk about it."

S. GROSS

DIARY OF A CAT

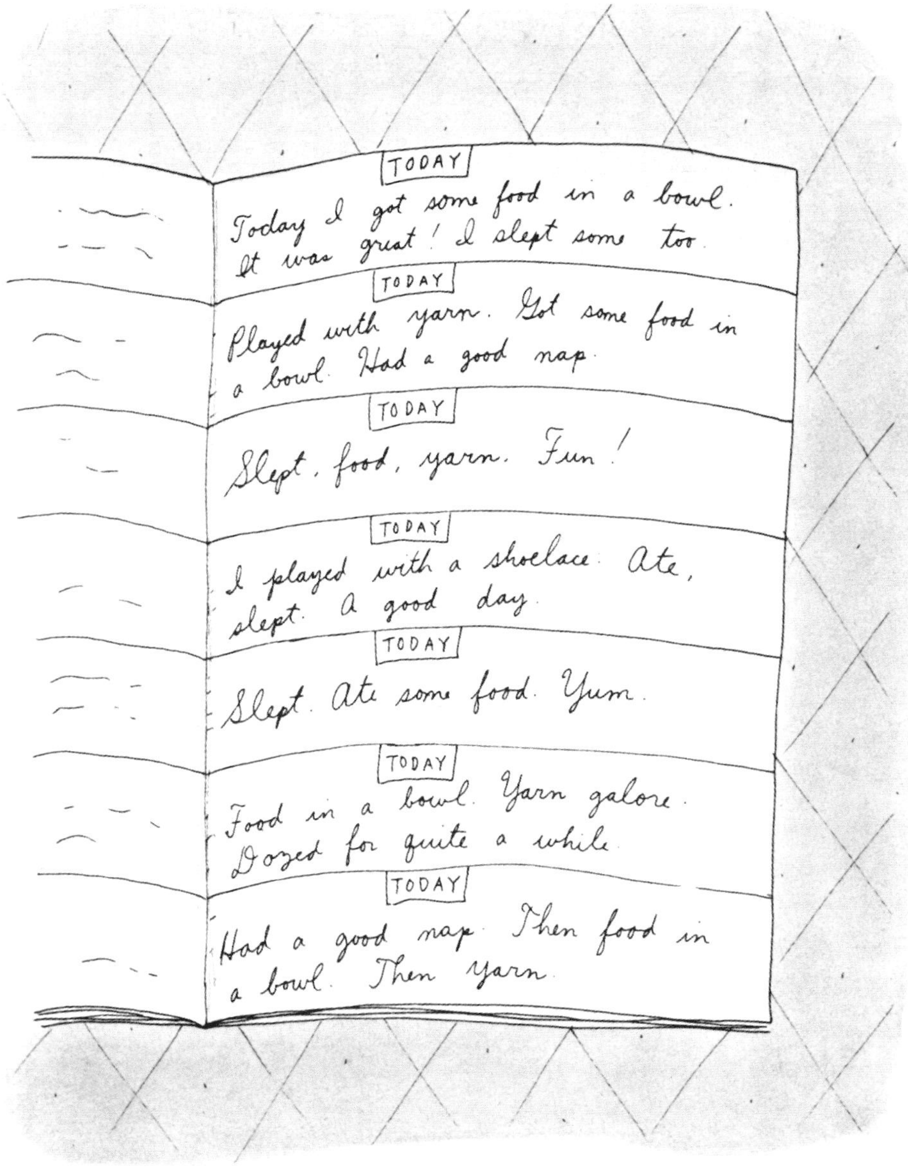
TODAY
Today I got some food in a bowl. It was great! I slept some too.
TODAY
Played with yarn. Got some food in a bowl. Had a good nap.
TODAY
Slept, food, yarn. Fun!
TODAY
I played with a shoelace. Ate, slept. A good day.
TODAY
Slept. Ate some food. Yum.
TODAY
Food in a bowl. Yarn galore. Dozed for quite a while.
TODAY
Had a good nap. Then food in a bowl. Then yarn.

"The fact that you cats were considered sacred in
ancient Egypt cuts no ice with me."

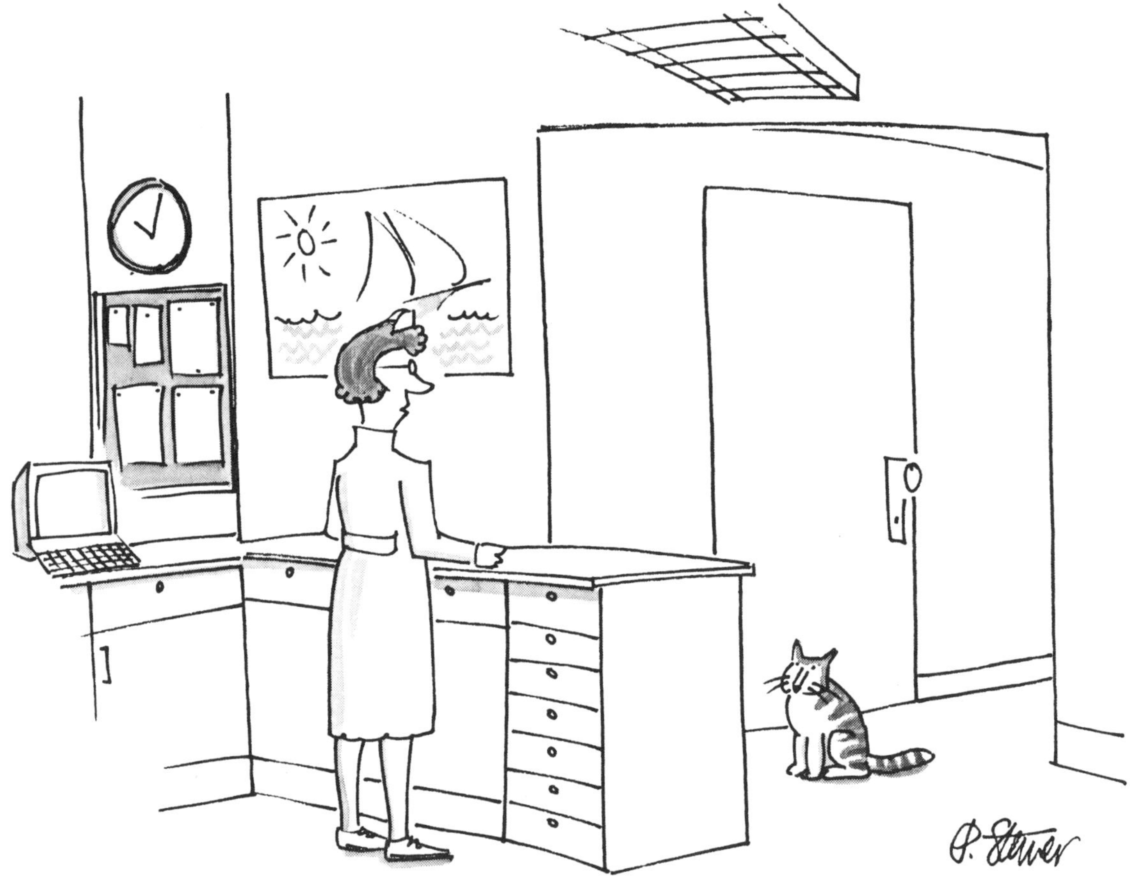
P. Steiner

"The patient in 12-C needs comforting."

"I distinctly heard a bark."

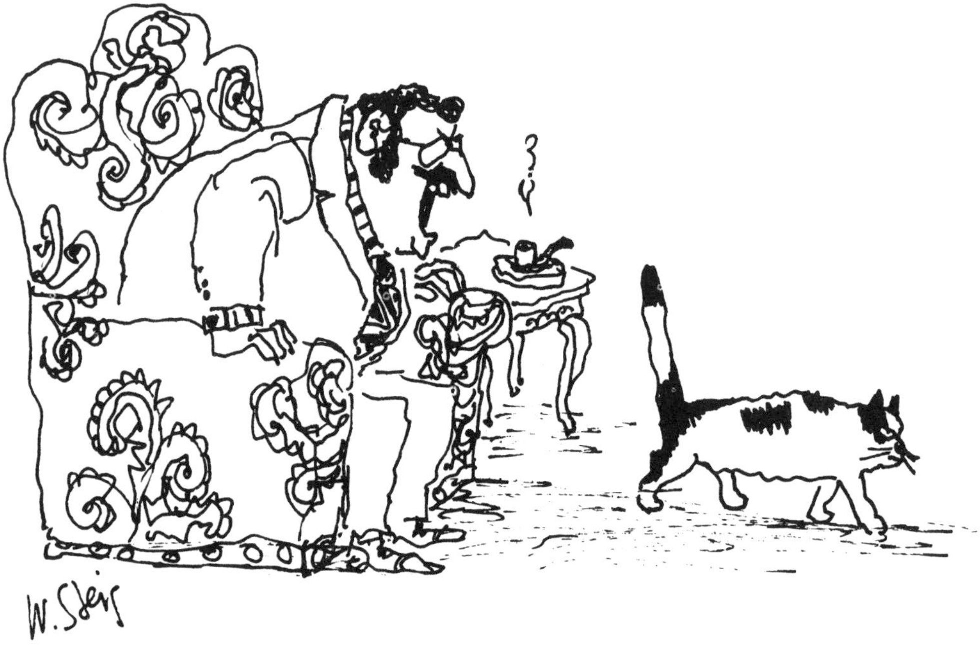
W. Steig

"And I can get along without you!"

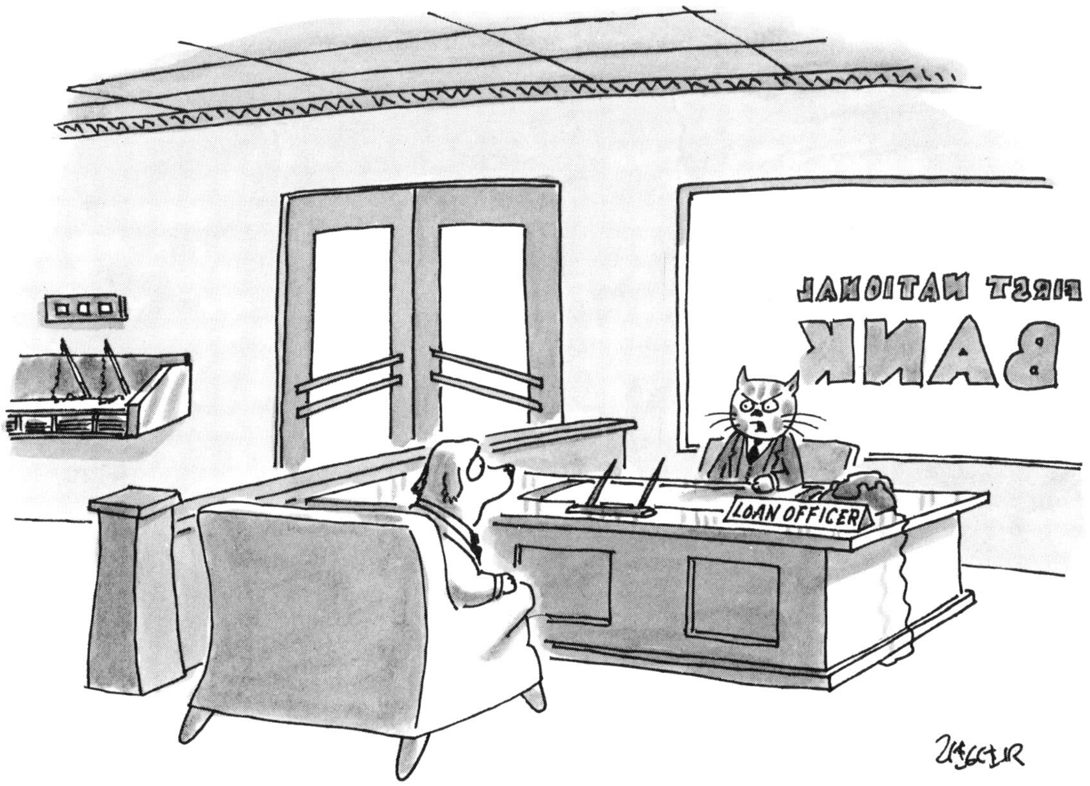
FIRST NATIONAL
BANK
LOAN OFFICER

"Beg."

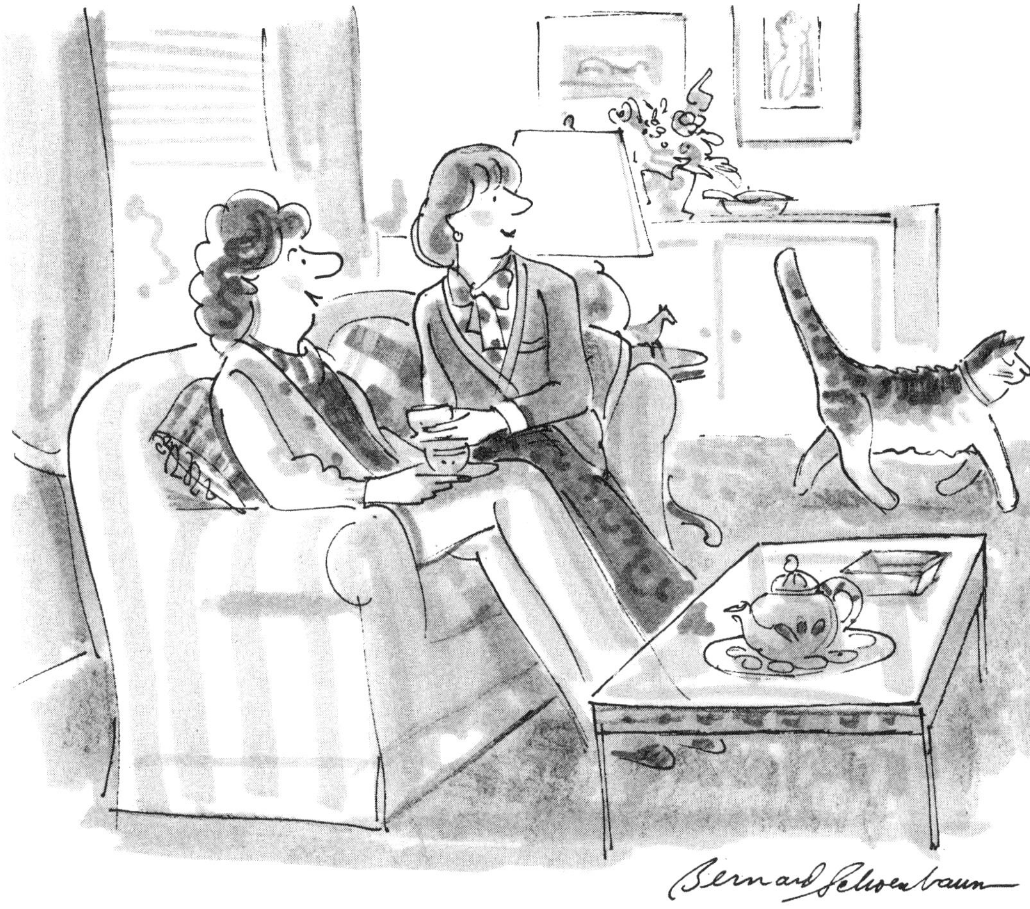
Bernard Schoenbaum

"She has her own agenda."

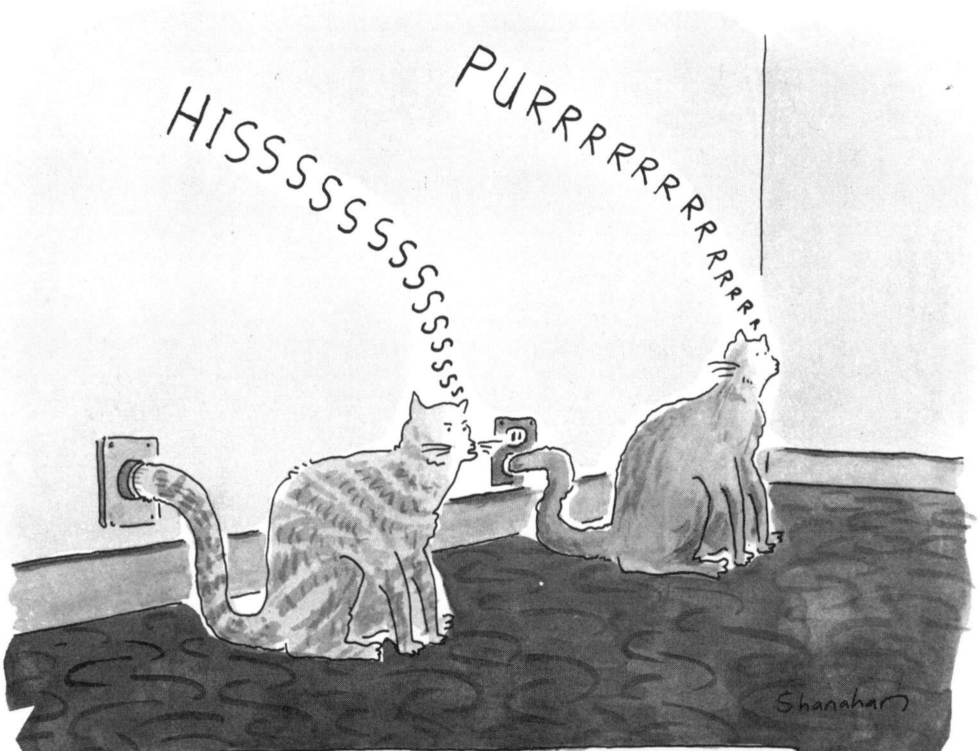
HISSSSSSSSSSSSSSSSS
PURRRRRRRRRRRRRRRR
Shanahan

GAS VS. ELECTRIC

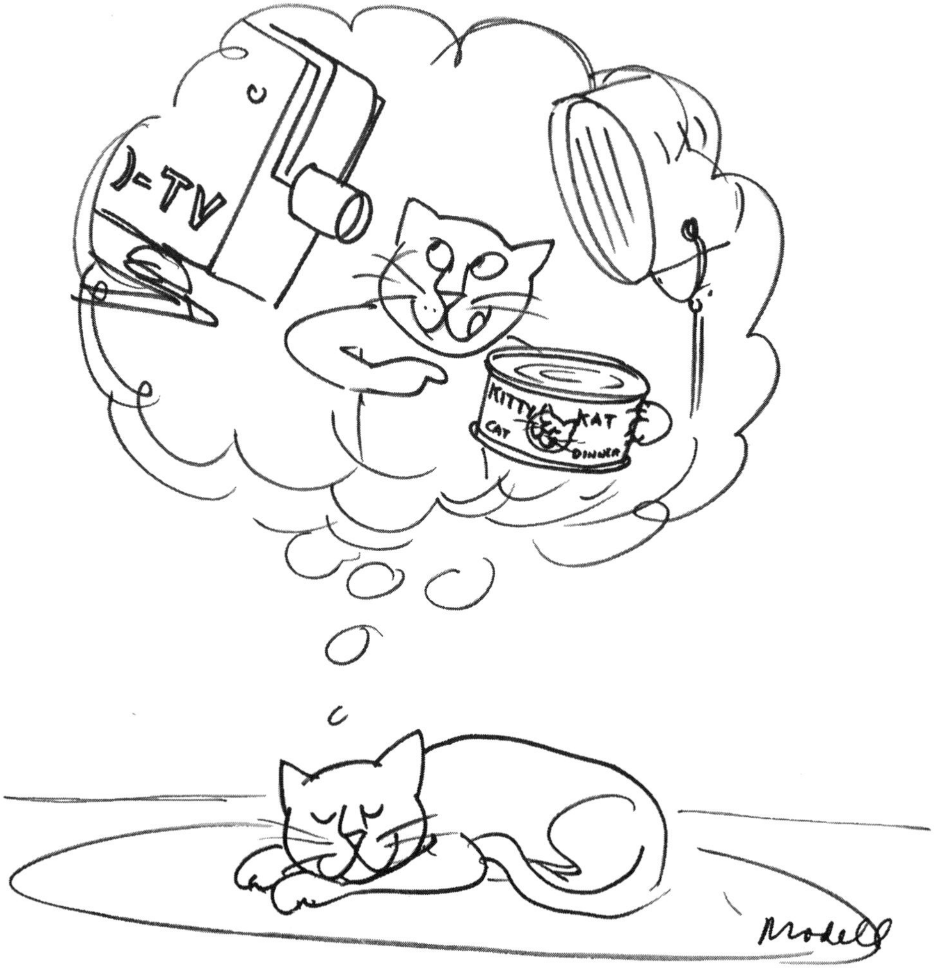
)-TV
KITTY KAT
CAT
DINNER
Modell

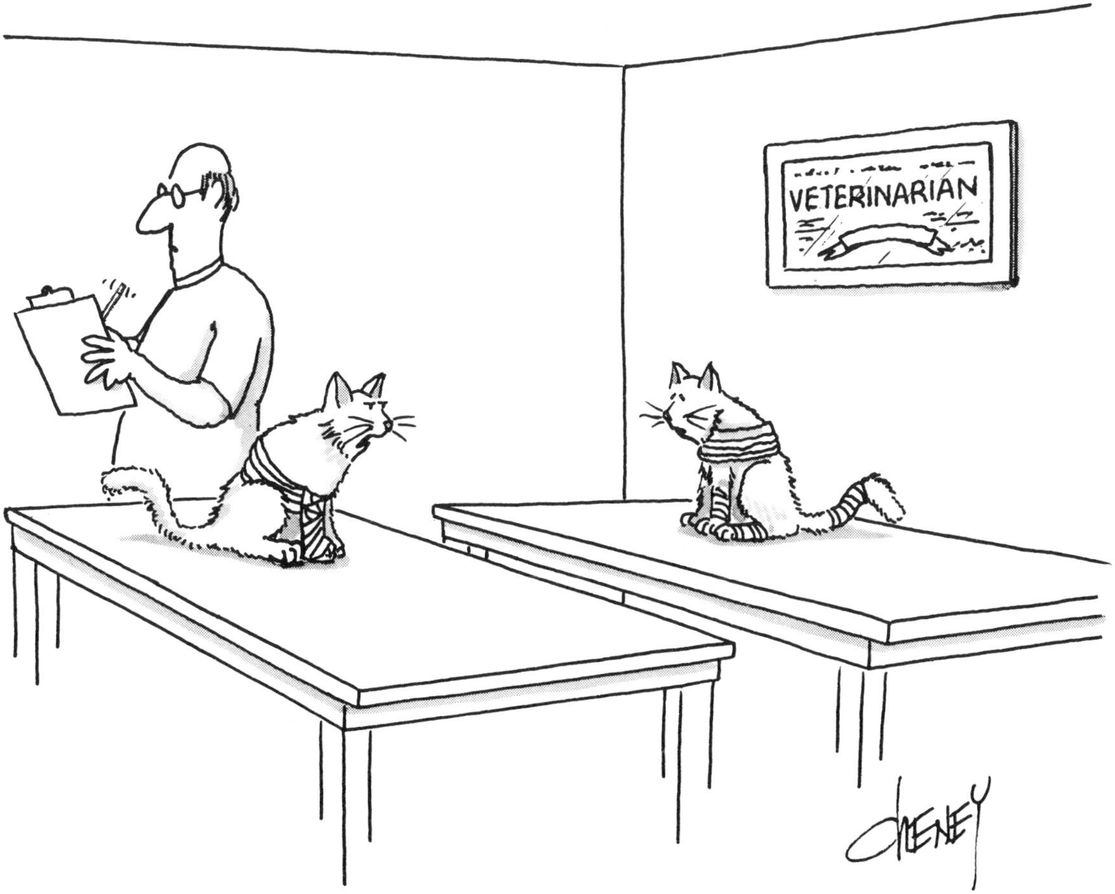
VETERINARIAN
CHENEY

"I tried to make it from the windowsill to the top of the refrigerator. How about you?"

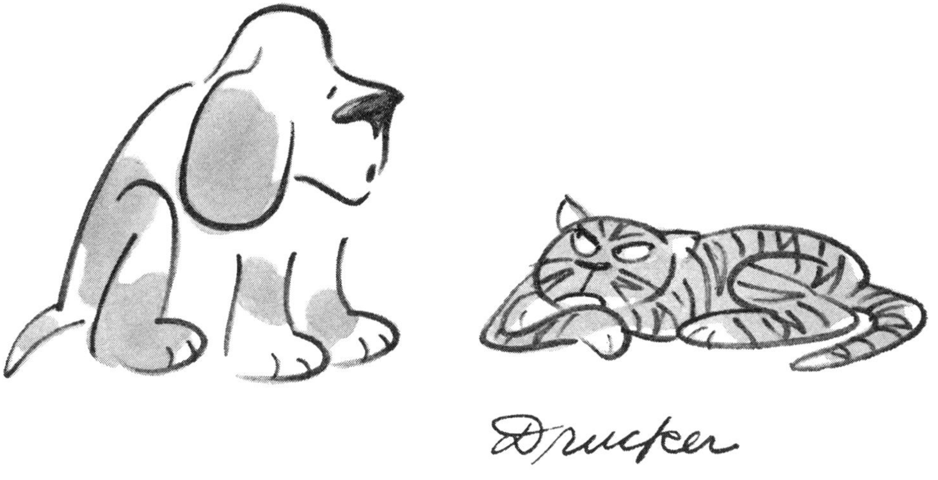
Drucker

"Well, sir, then I take it you would vote for any cat in preference to a capable dog."

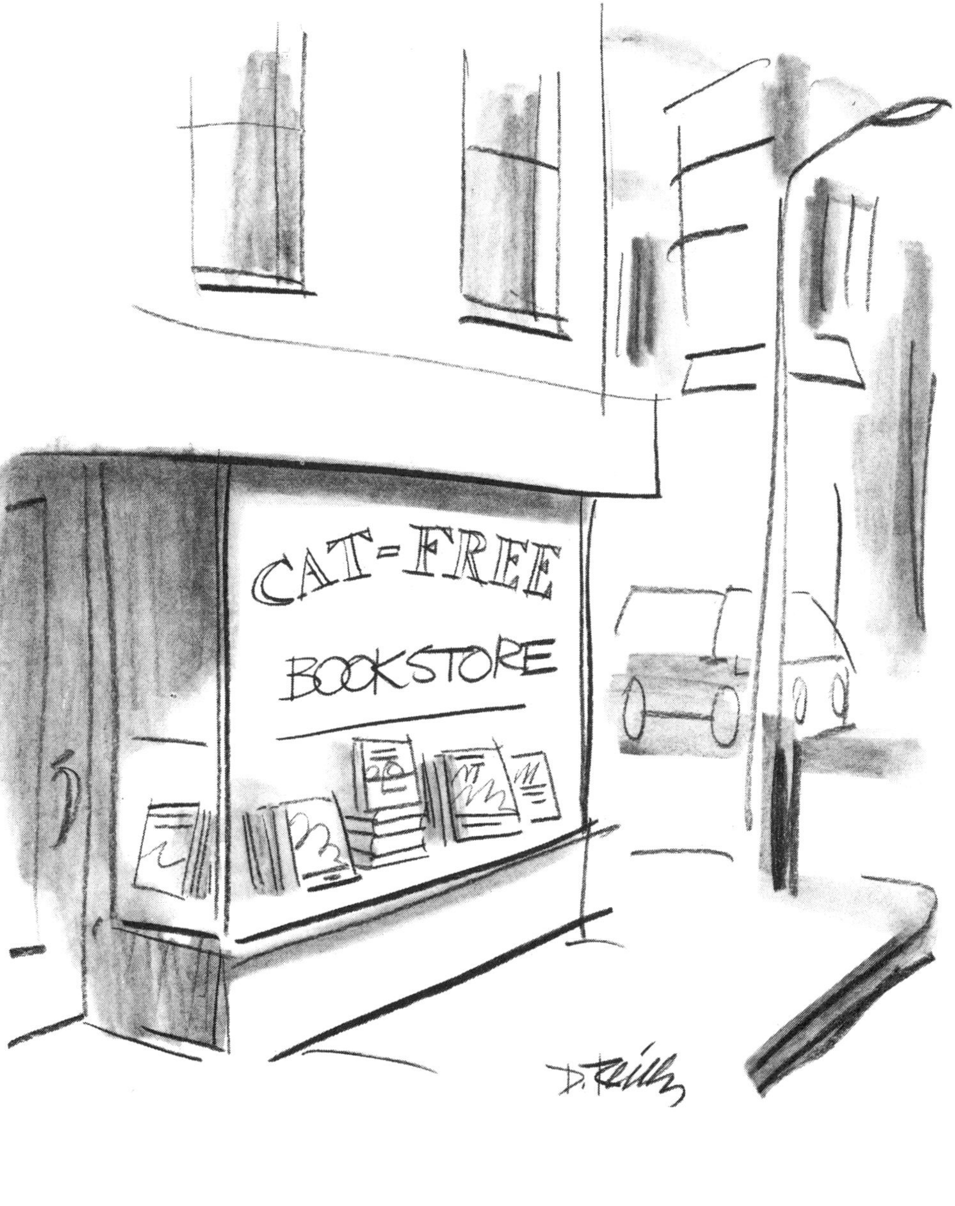
CAT-FREE
BOOKSTORE
D. Reilly

"*I believe I've earned the right to your respect.*"

"*Do you think a Siamese cat could tip it over?*"

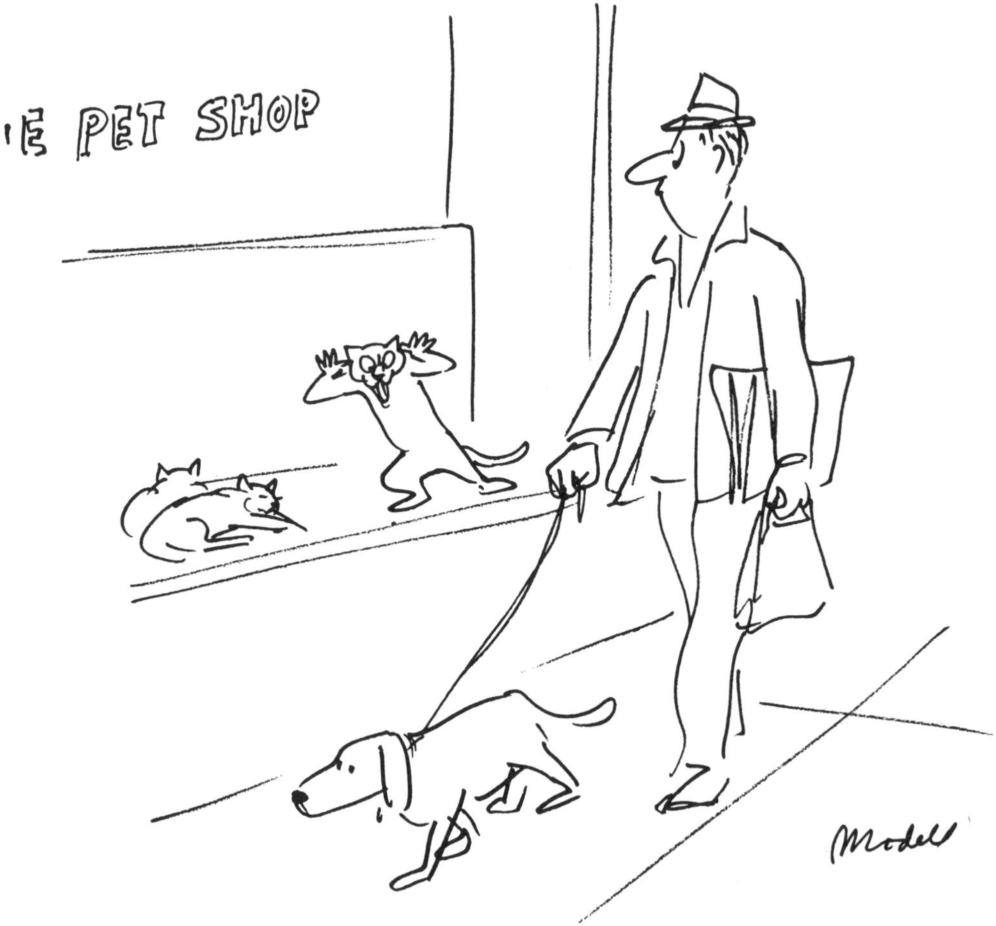
'E PET SHOP
Modell

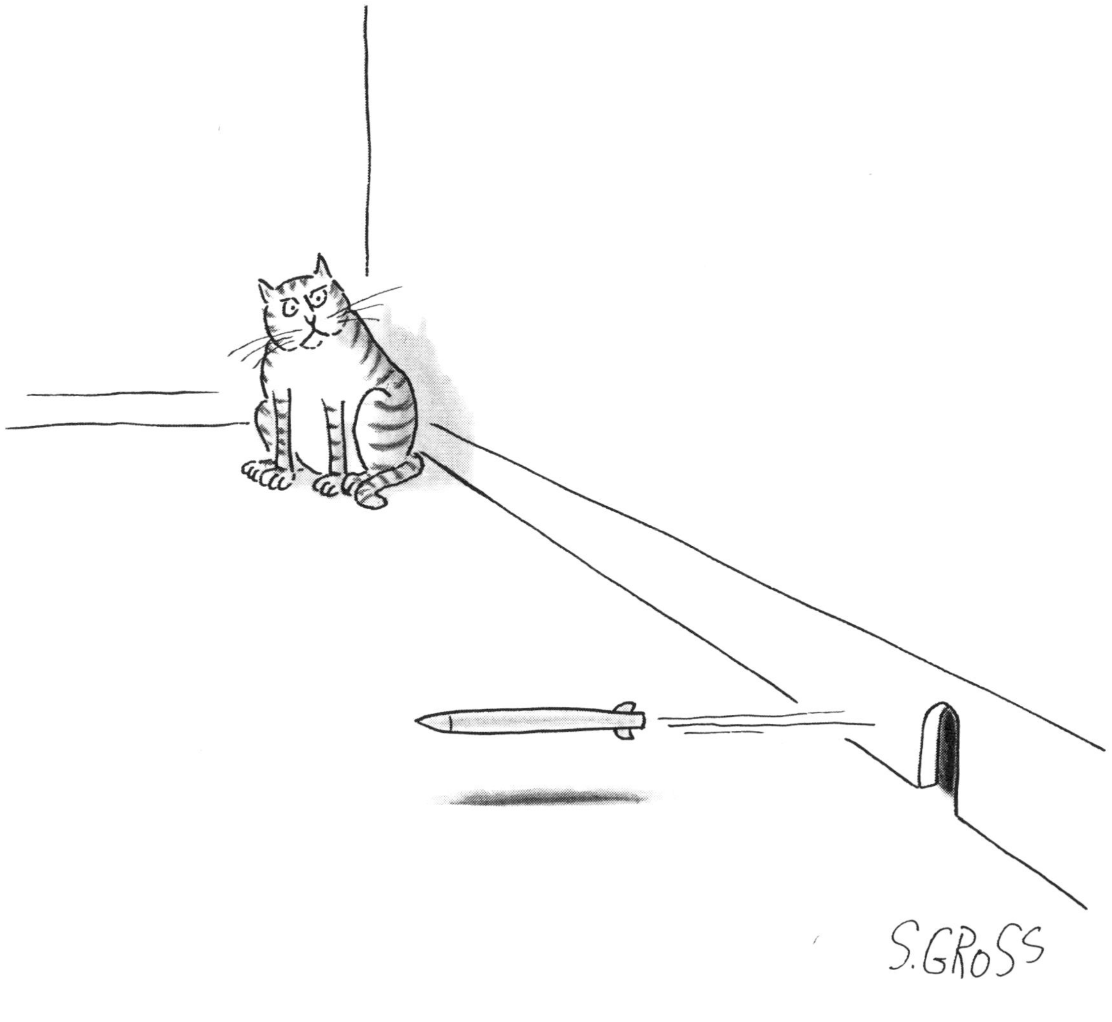
S.GROSS

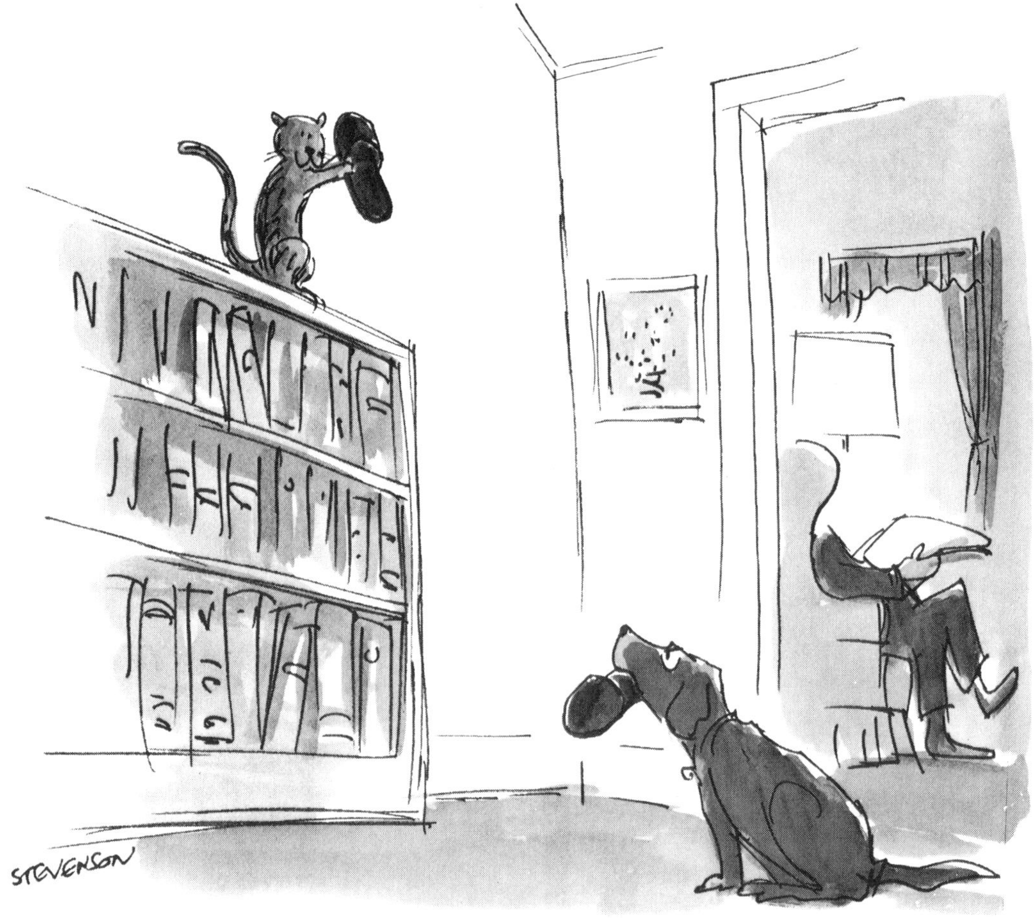
STEVENSON

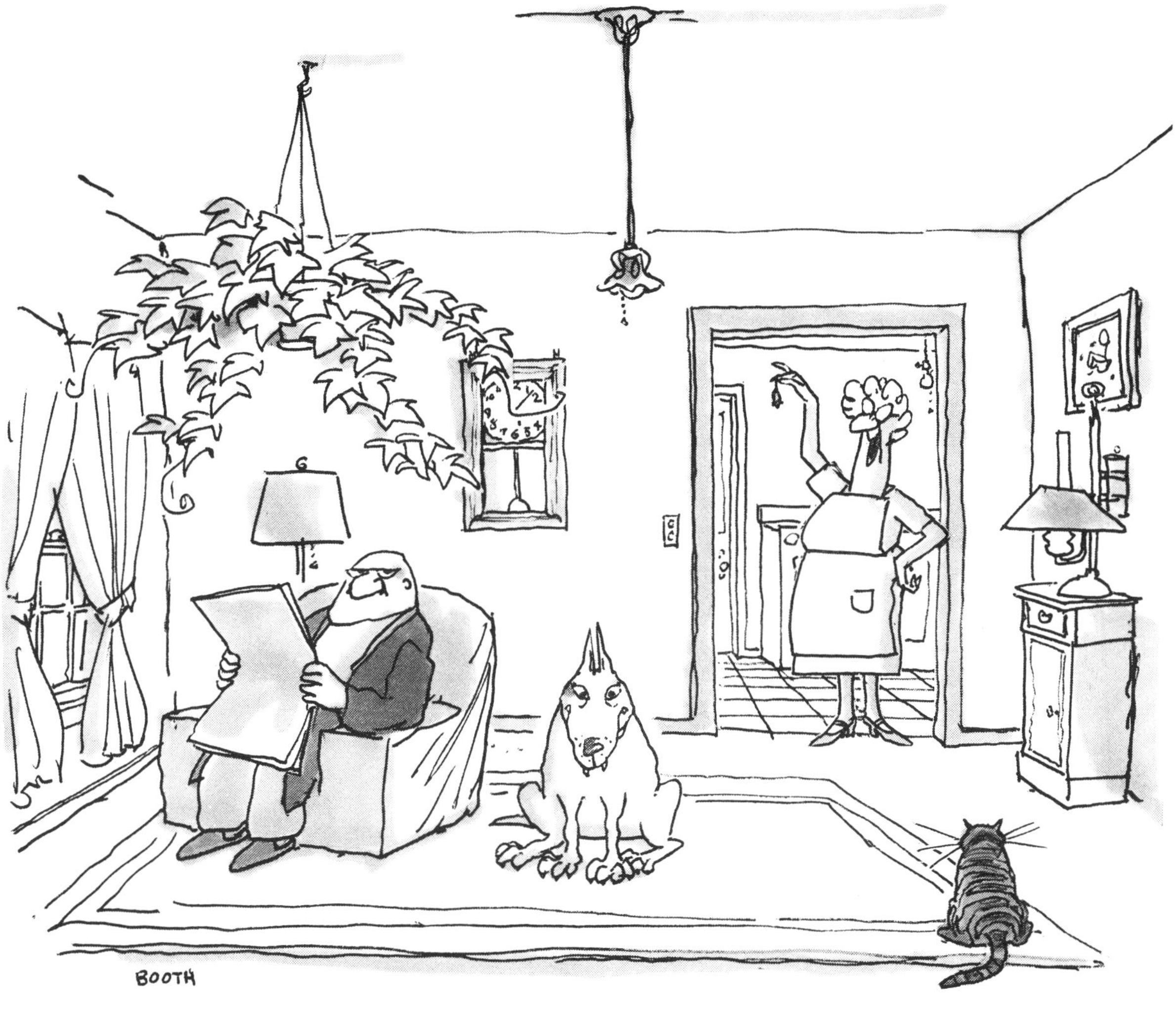
BOOTH

"And whose little mole is this?"

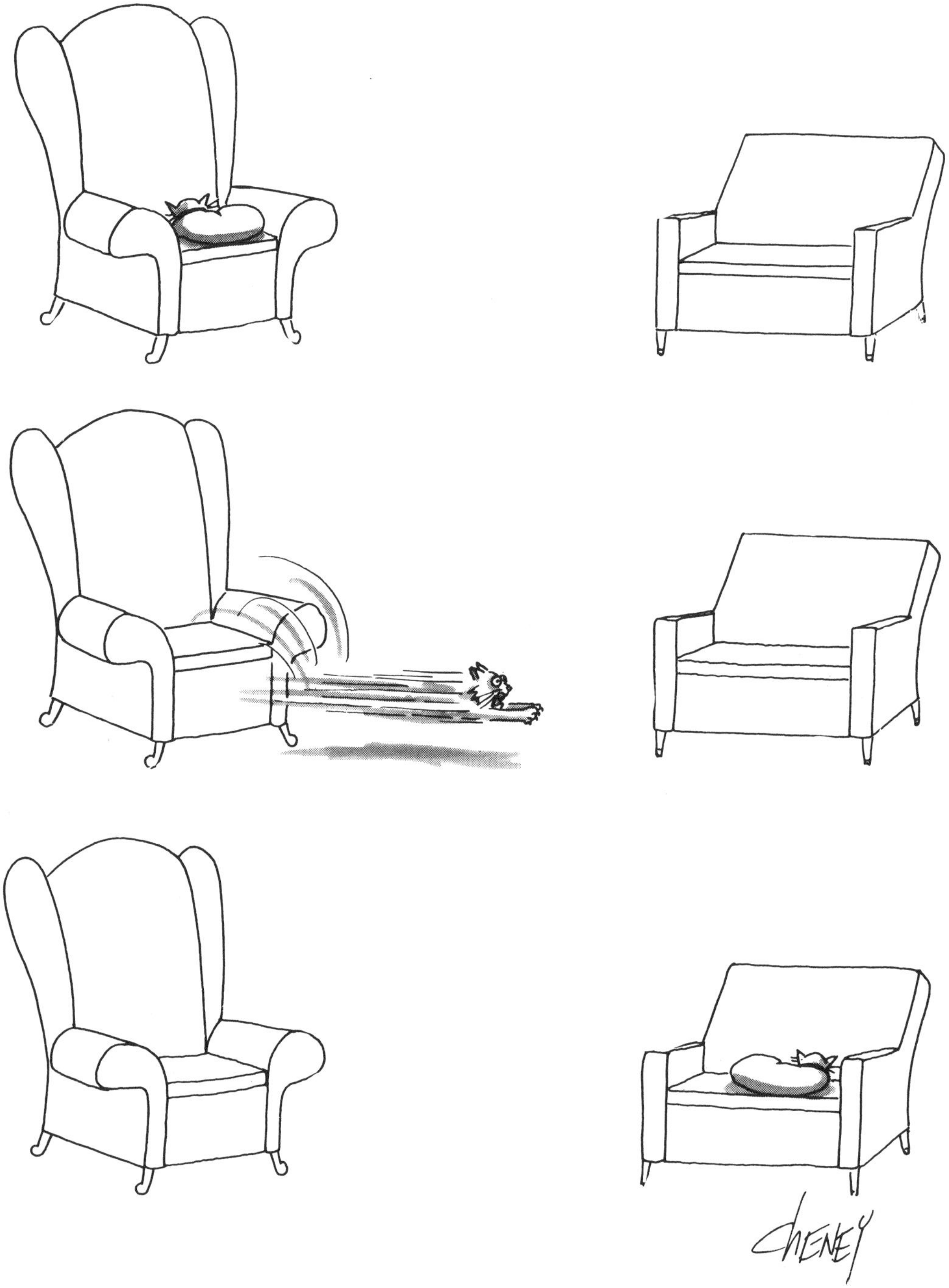
CHENEY

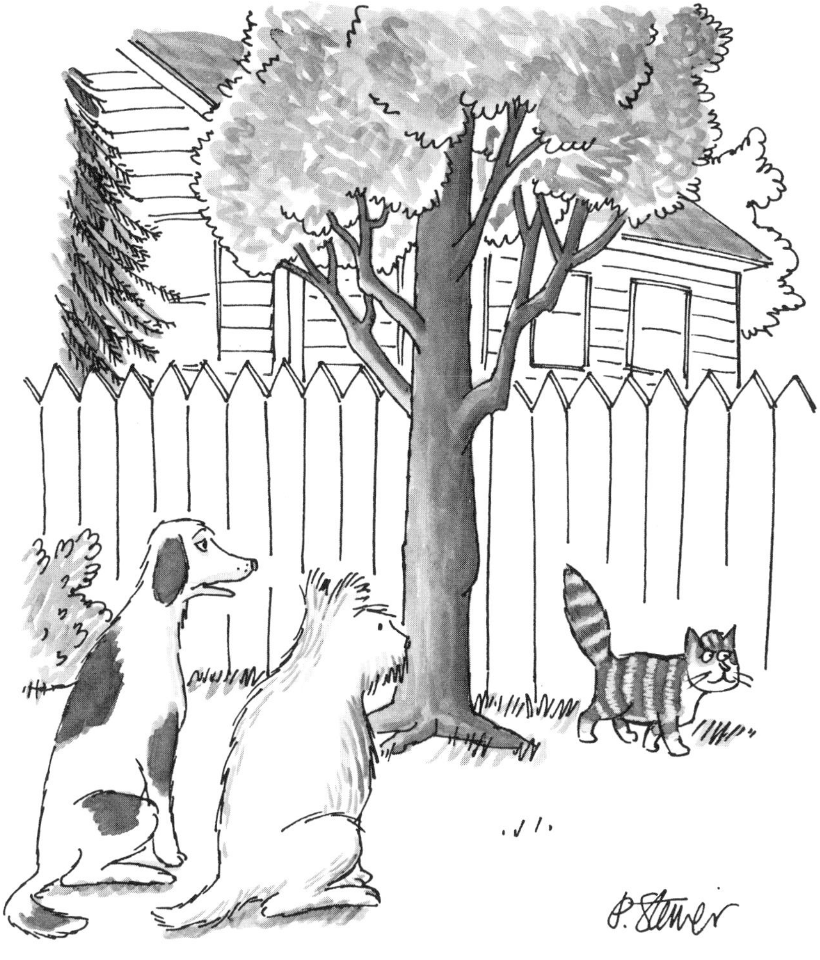
P. Steiner

"What do cats want?"

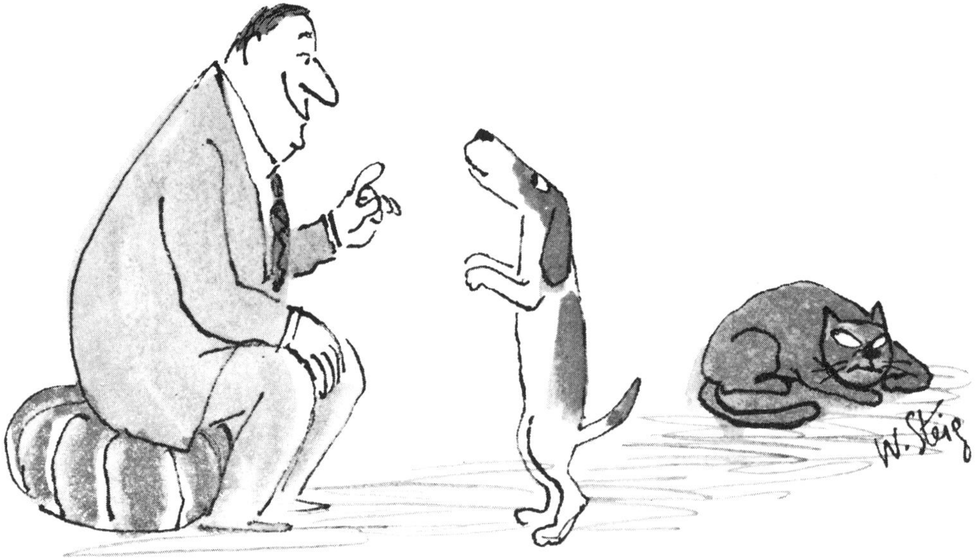
W. Steig

"We have fourteen cats, but Kevin thinks we only have twelve."

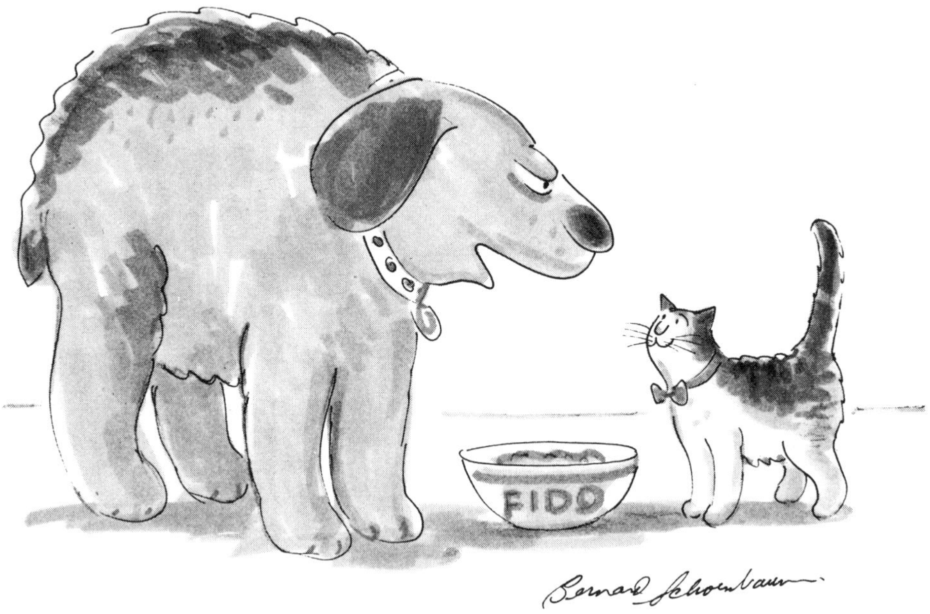
FIDO

"Don't get cute with me."

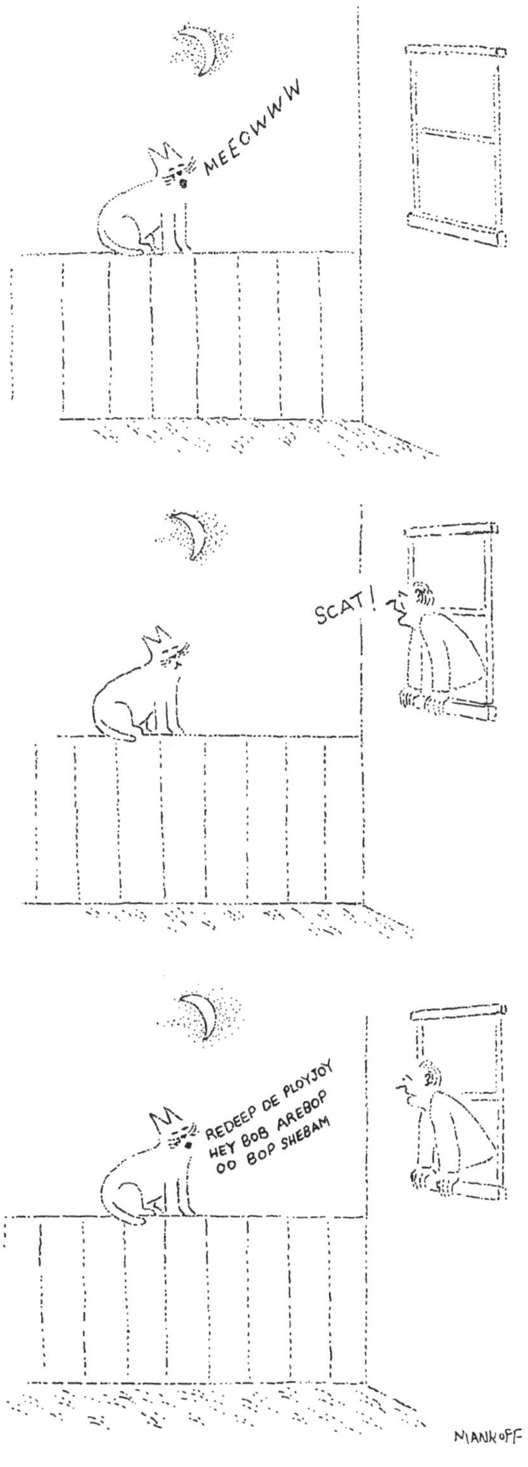
MEEOWWW
SCAT!
REDEEP DE PLOYJOY
HEY BOB AREBOP
OO BOP SHEBAM
MANKOFF

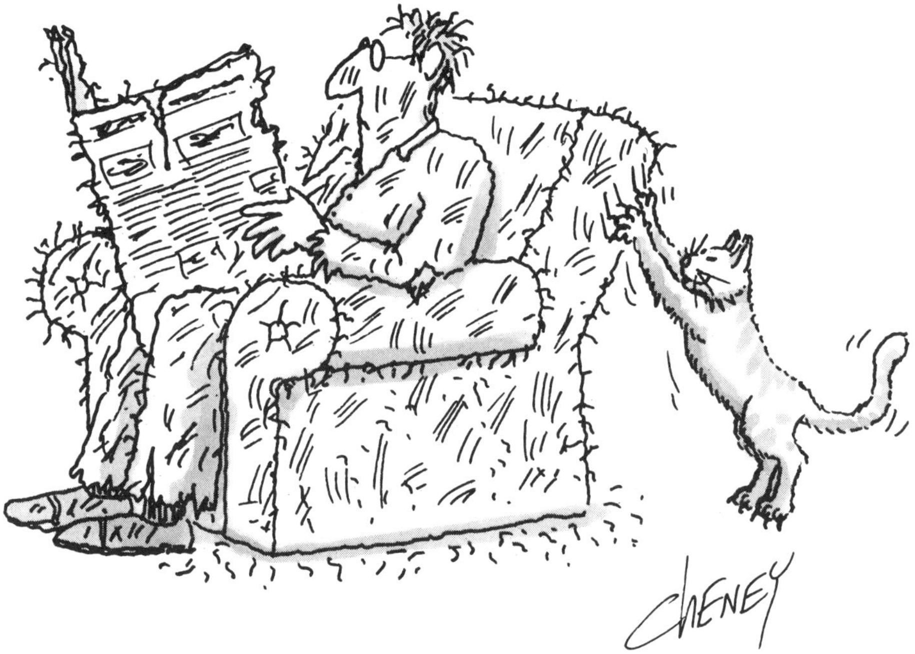
CHENEY

Scaredy-Cats

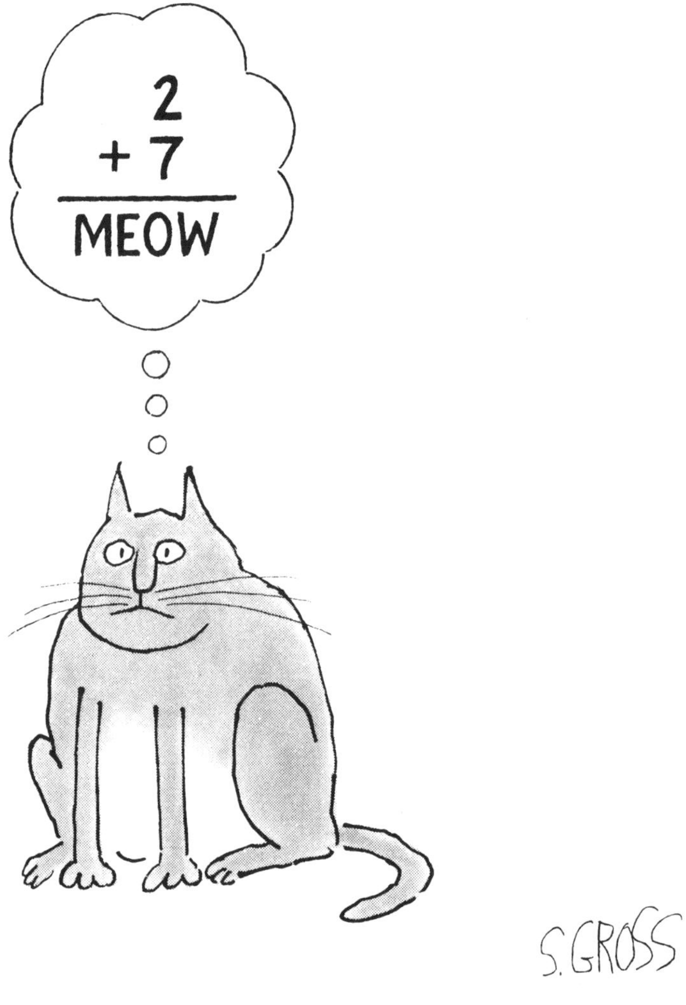
2
+ 7
MEOW
S. GROSS

CATS ARE NOT AS INTELLIGENT AS YOU THINK.

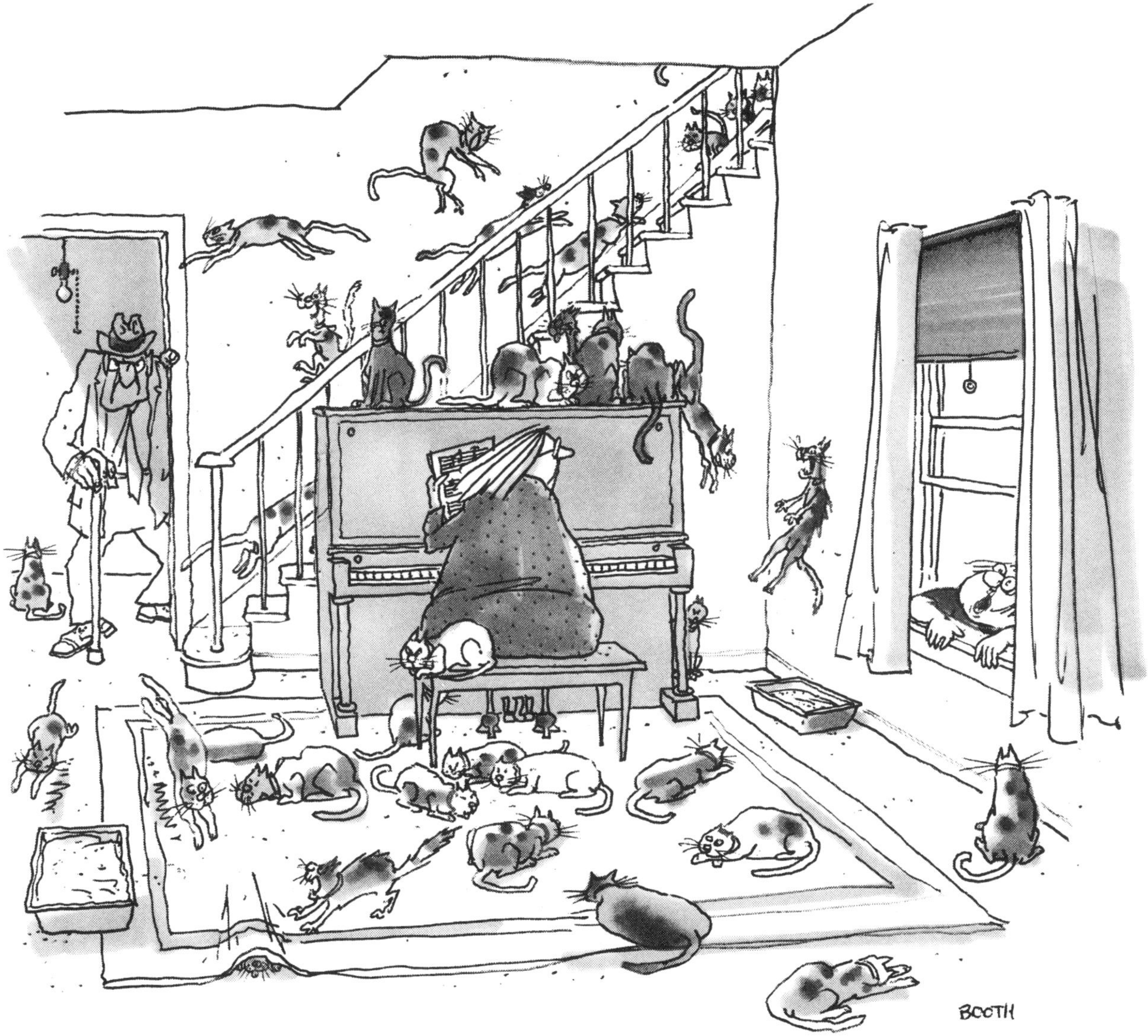
BOOTH

*"Glendora Hagan got in another load of cats,
Elinor honey. Can you take a couple?"*

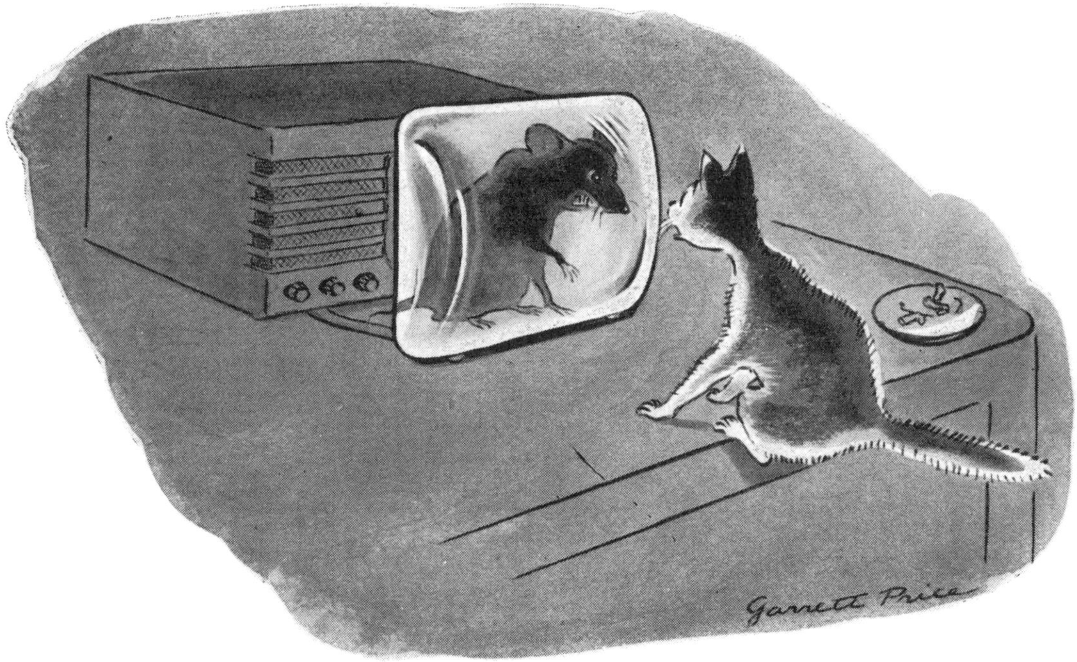
Garrett Price

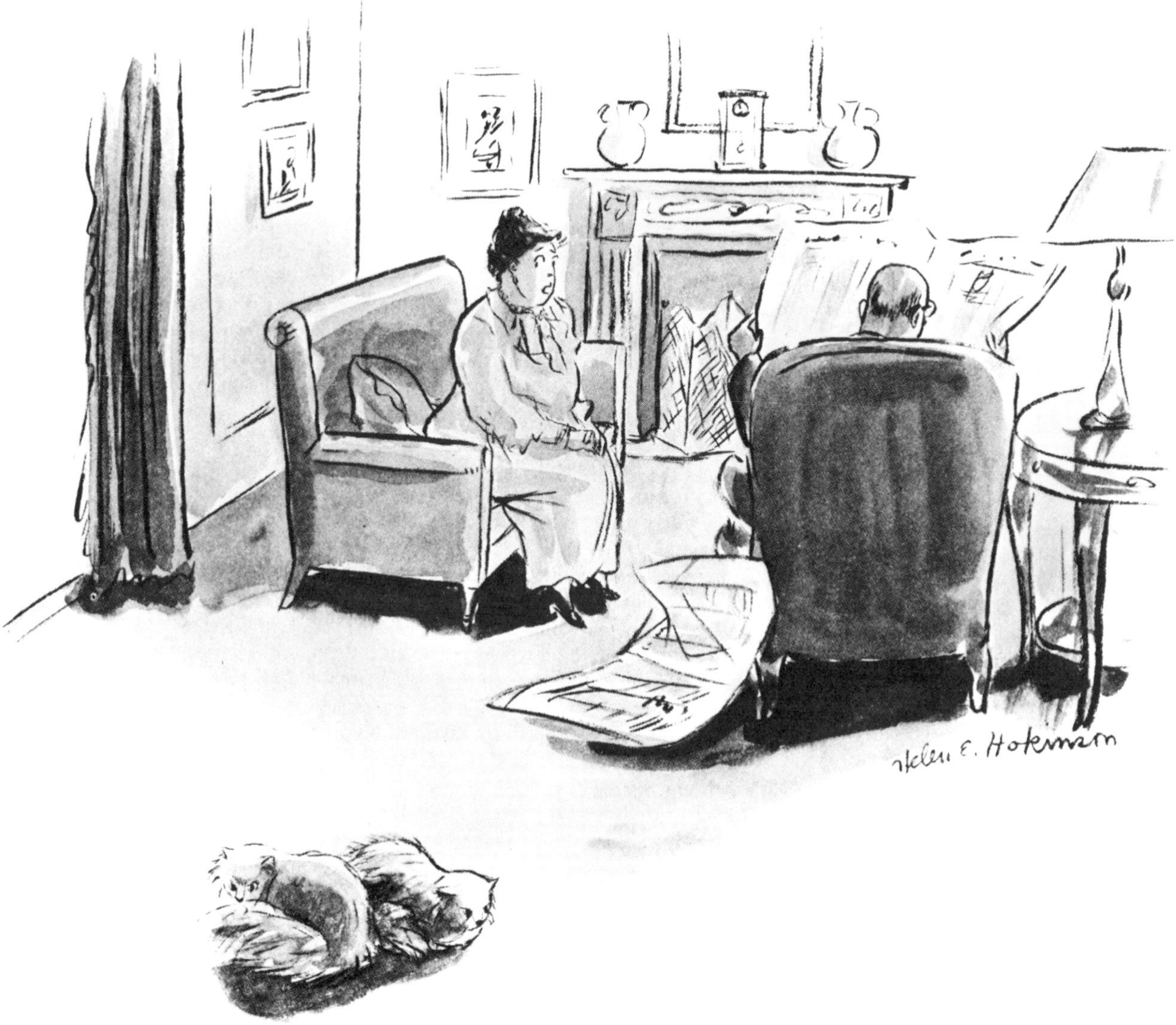

"Both cats are mad at me."

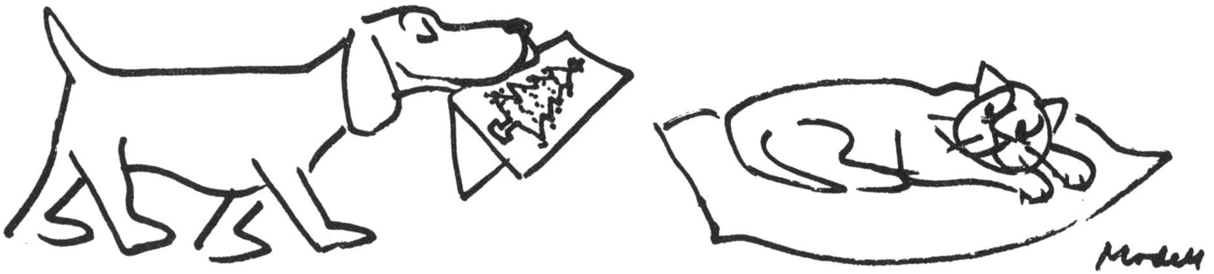
Modell

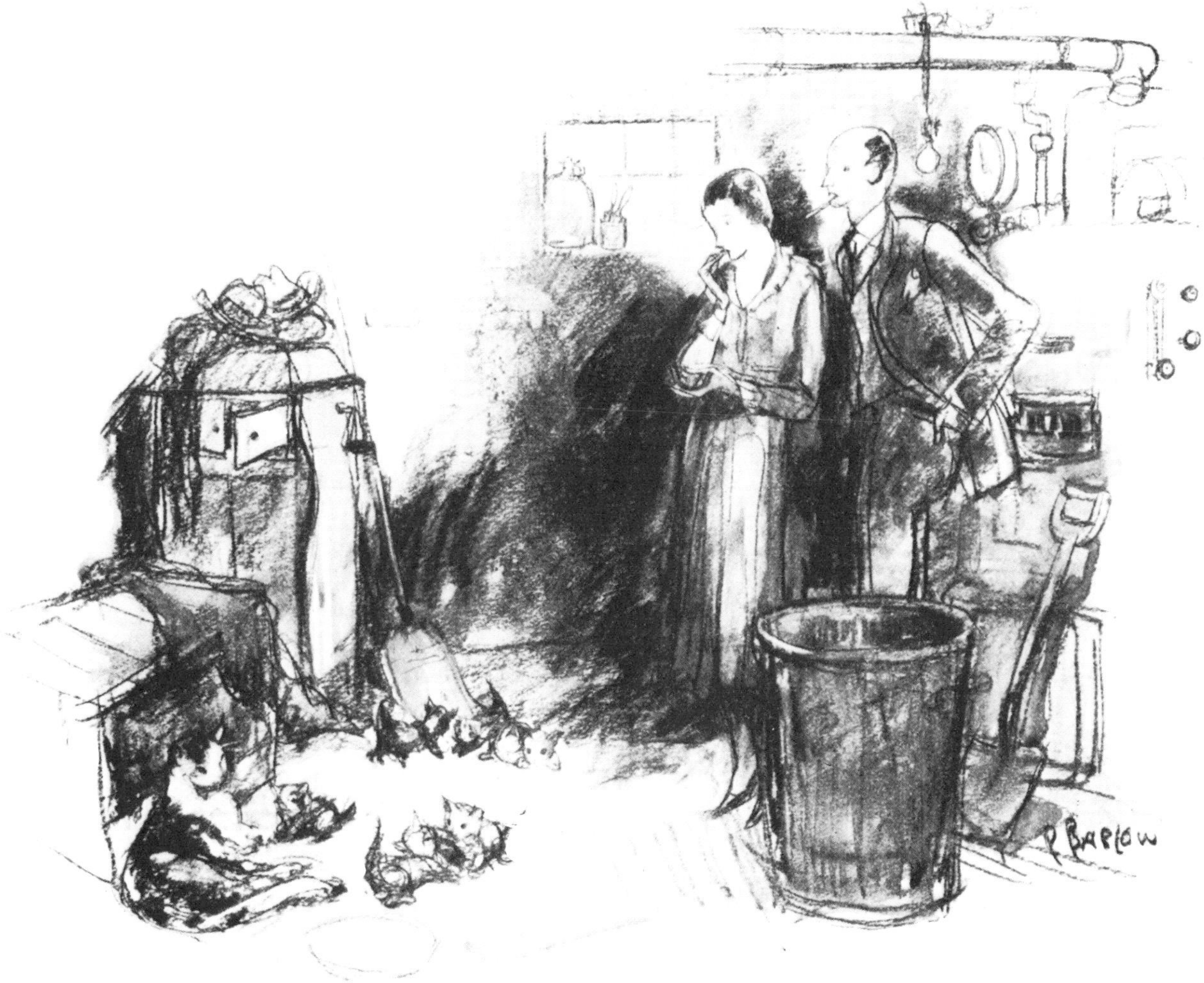
R. BARLOW

"Now let's see—there's the Brosnahans, Mrs. Waldo, Arthur Elder, the man at the A. & P. store. Now I wonder about Hannah Carpenter."

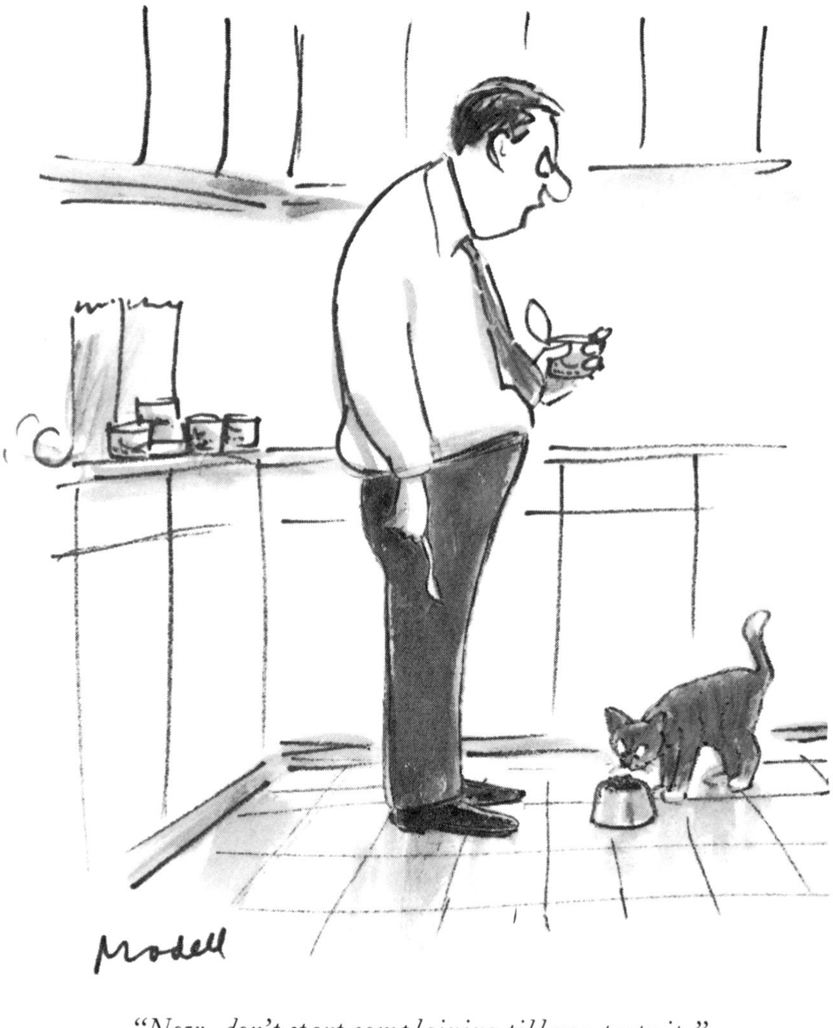
Modell

"Now, don't start complaining till you taste it."

"I said you're in my light."

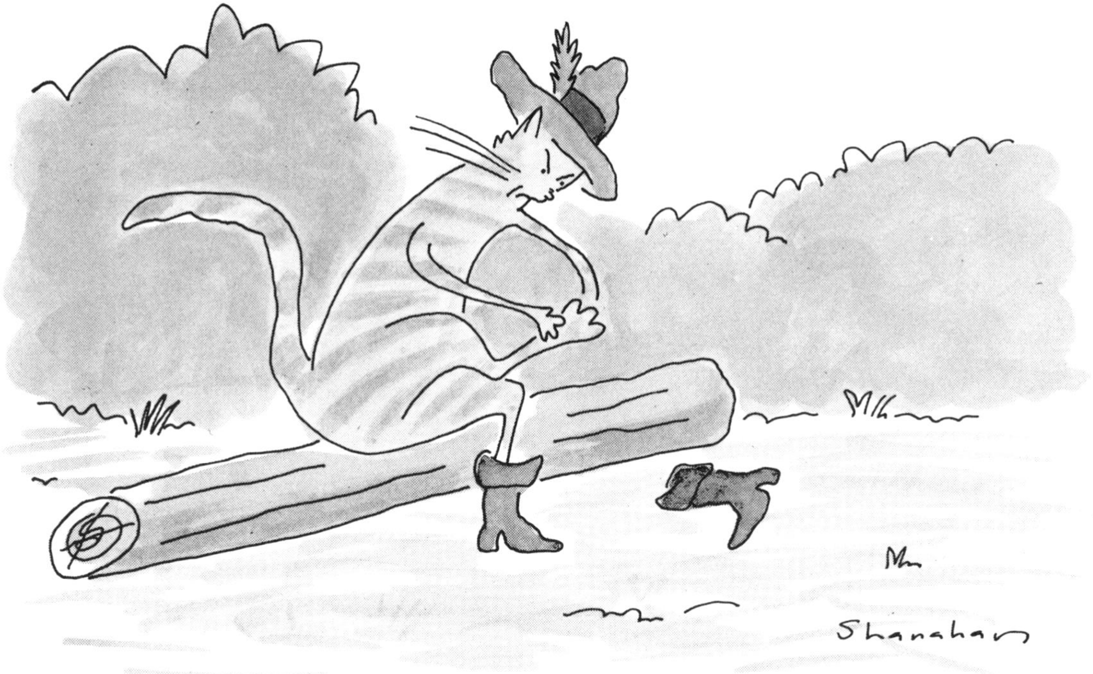
Shanahan

PUSS IN FACTORY SECONDS

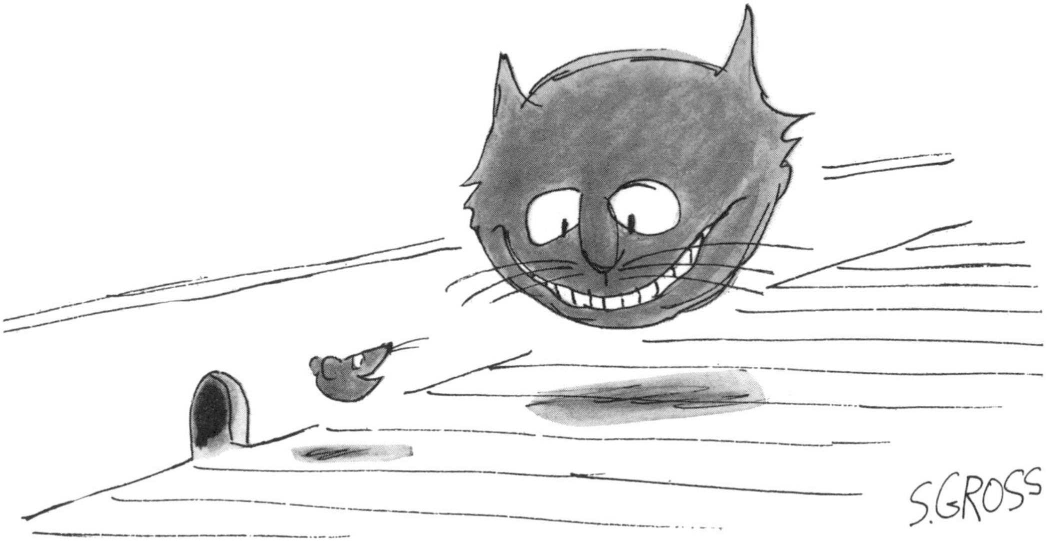
S.GROSS

"I'm a Cheshire mouse."

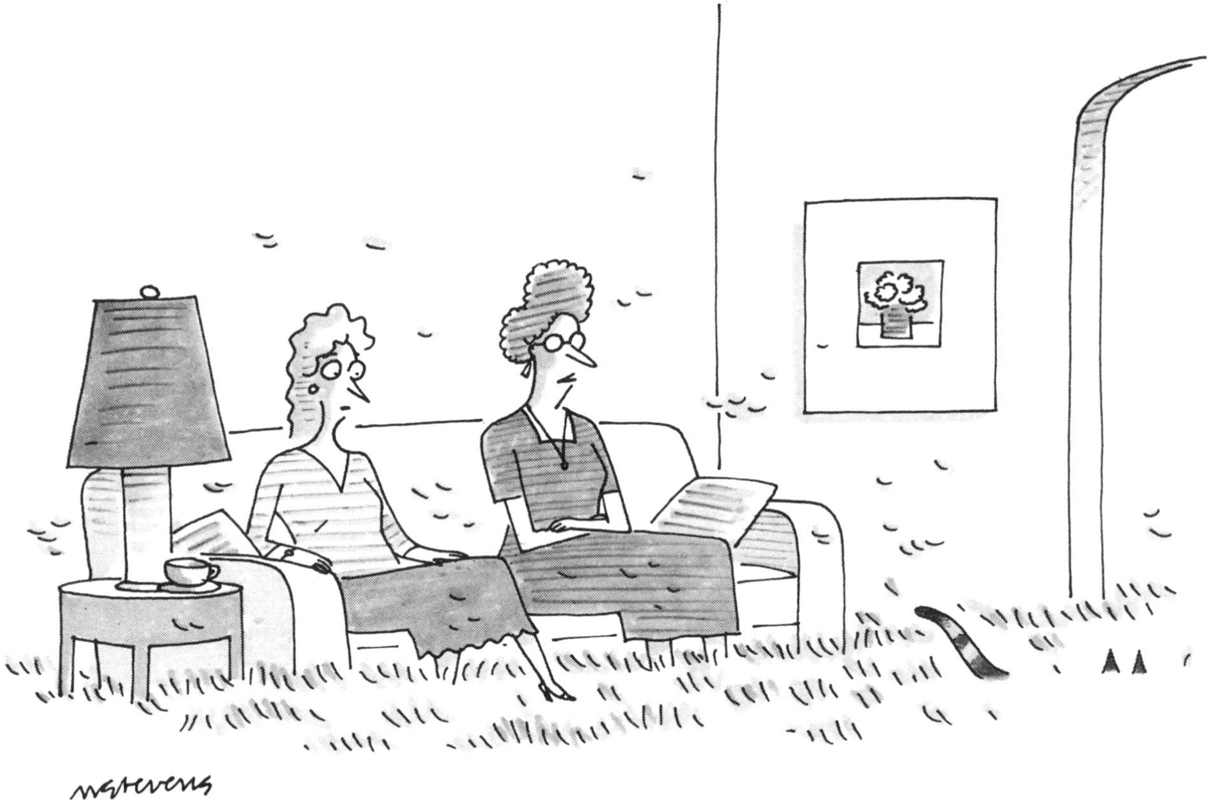
mstevens

"Muffie's shedding."

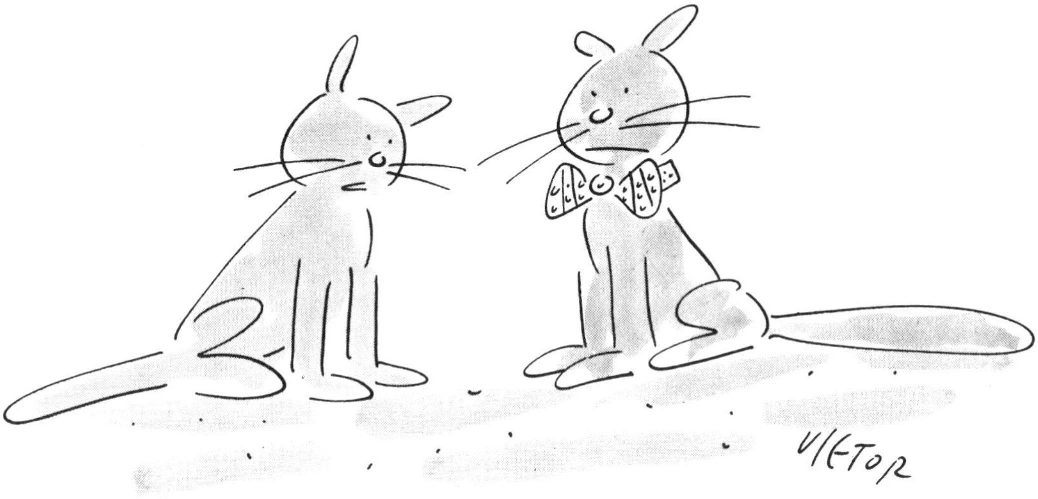
VICTOR

"I'm sorry, but I think it's uncatlike."

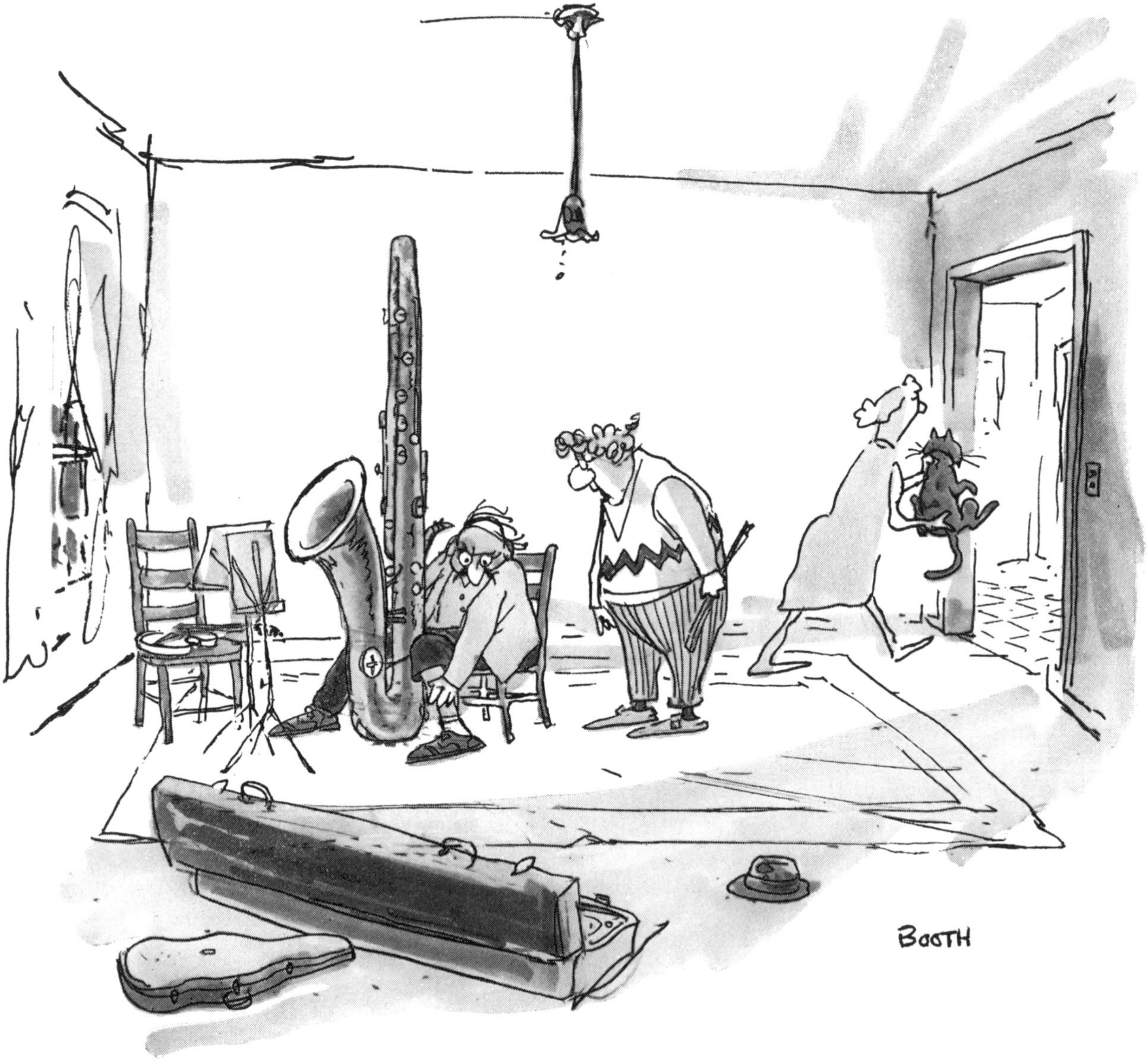
BOOTH

"I do apologize, Rinehart. The cat has never bitten anyone previously."

"Hey, pal, let's hear 'Doggie in the Window' again, and this time play it like you mean it!"

"Miss Egan, bring me everything we have on cats."

Index of Artists

The text of this book was set in Caslon Old Face No. 2 at Kennedy
Typographers, New York, New York. Printed and bound by Halliday
Lithographers, West Hanover, Massachusetts.
Designed by Virginia Tan.